•CreaTive KiDS•

20th century QUIZ BOOK

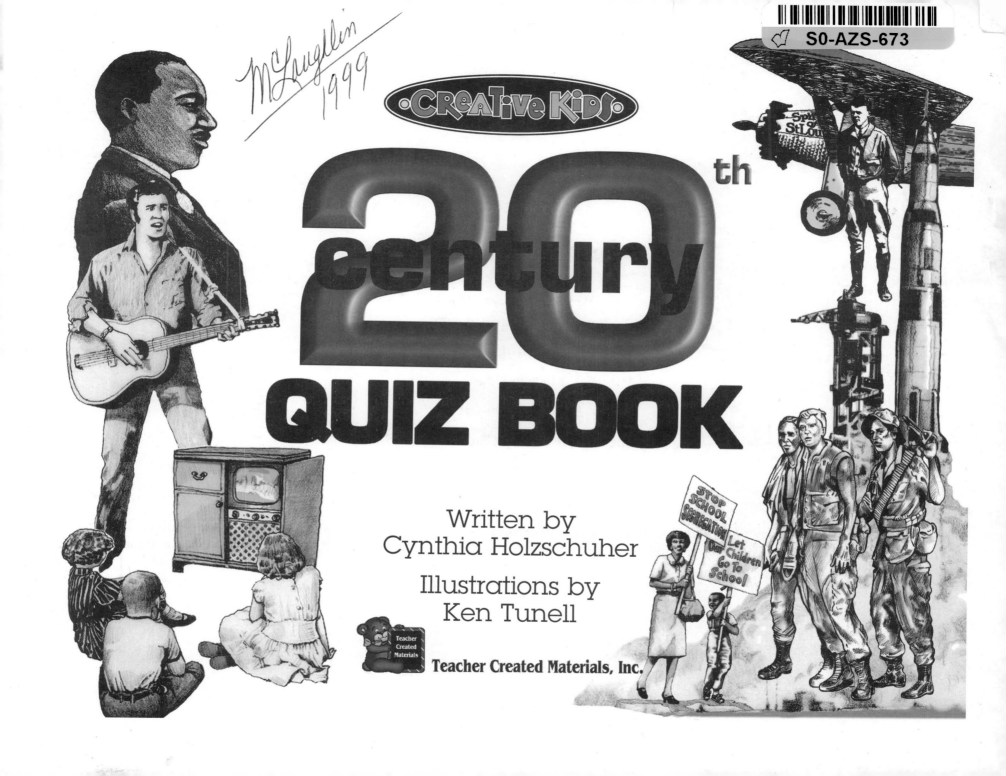

Written by
Cynthia Holzschuher

Illustrations by
Ken Tunell

Teacher Created Materials, Inc.

Teacher Created Materials, Inc.

6421 Industry Way

Westminster, CA 92683

www.teachercreated.com

©1999 Teacher Created Materials, Inc.

Made in U.S.A.

ISBN-1-57690-601-9

Library of Congress Catalog Card Number: 99-62415

Editor:

Walter Kelly, M. A.

1900	1910	1920	1930	1940	1950	1960	1970	1980	1990

Table of Contents

Introduction

The Creative Kids series provides ways to exercise and develop brain power! Each page stands alone and can be used as a quick and easy filler activity. The activities are especially useful in helping children to develop the following assets:

- logic and other thinking skills
- research skills
- spelling skills
- general vocabulary and knowledge

Creative Kids: 20th Century Quiz Book can be used in conjunction with TCM 2100 (*The 20th Century*), or answers can be found in any current encyclopedia or reference book, like *Chronicle of the 20th Century* (Dorling Kindersley, 1995). Some of the puzzles include a word bank for children who may need assistance completing the page. If you wish to make the puzzles more difficult, you may block out or fold the word banks under before duplicating.

These materials can be used with any social studies curriculum to introduce and reinforce knowledge. Current, accurate data has been used in this book as much as possible. We hope you and your children will have great fun learning more about the people and events of the 20th century by using the activities in this Creative Kids book.

Mother's Day

This holiday to honor mothers was first celebrated on a large scale on May 10, 1908. Read the clues and write the answers in the blanks. Then unscramble the letters in the circles and use them to answer the question.

1. mother's gender

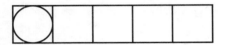

2. season for this holiday

3. country where "Mothering Sunday" originated

4. traditional Mother's Day flower

5. Who was the president who signed a resolution to make Mother's Day a national holiday?

6. Rearrange the letters in these words to reveal the name of the founder of Mother's Day.

SIN   **JAVA**   **RAN**

— — — — — — — — — —

4

Memory Game

Study the picture for three minutes. Then, put it out of sight. On another sheet of paper, list as many items from the picture as you can remember.

Who's Driving?

The first mass-produced automobile, the Model T, made its debut in 1908. It outsold all other cars for 20 years. Over 15 million Model Ts had been made when it was discontinued in 1927. Today, a car's license plate can tell something about its driver. Decode the following plates. Which important figures from the decade of 1900 to 1909 might be driving cars with these license plates?

1. GR8 WRTR _____

2. 2 XPLRS _____ _____

3. NO BOOZ _____

4. BIG BUX _____

5. GR8 RTST _____

6. US PRES _____

7. 1ST LADY _____

8. FLY BROS _____ _____

9. BRIT HRM _____

10. 4N LDR _____

11. 2 4 MINOA _____

12. CAR MKR _____

6

Analogies

To complete an analogy, you must first determine the relationship between the given items. The relationship may be person to birthplace, place to event, inventor to invention, etc. They are read as follows:

Du Bois:NAACP::Robert Baden-Powell:Boy Scouts

(Du Bois is to the NAACP as Robert Baden-Powell is to the Boy Scouts)

1. Wright Brothers:airplane::Henry Ford:_____

2 Susan B. Anthony:suffrage::Carry Nation:_____

3. William McKinley:Ohio::Theodore Roosevelt:_____

4. Davis Cup:tennis::World Cup:_____

5. dirigible:airship::_____:armored landship

6. Einstein:Germany::Pavlov:_____

7. Planck:quantum theory::_____:theory of relativity

8. Rudyard Kipling:*The Jungle Book*::Beatrix Potter:_____

9. Picasso:_____::Cassatt:Impressionism

10. Edison:kinetophone::Marconi:_____

11. Anna Jarvis:Mother's Day::Sonora Dodd:_____

12. United States:_____::Australia:Aborigines

13. cricket:England::baseball:_____

14. Boer War:South Africa::Boxer Rebellion:_____

15. Charlie Gibson:fashion design::Florenz Ziegfield:_____

Ivan Pavlov

Rudyard Kipling

Presidential Diplomacy

Theodore Roosevelt was the first president to travel to a foreign country while in office. He was responsible for the construction of the Panama Canal. Circle every third letter in the puzzle box to reveal the West African proverb that explained Teddy Roosevelt's foreign policy. Write the message on the lines below.

```
Ⓢ  A  B  P  Y  V  E  K  T  A  R  Y  K
J  Y  S  D  K  O  B  C  F  I  D  T  C
W  L  O  X  Y  W  N  A  V  I  N  X  S
D  P  J  C  E  R  A  P  H  R  O  U  R
M  O  Y  H  C  A  P  O  B  Y  R  I  F
C  G  V  F  S  I  U  T  M  O  I  B  D
C  L  J  K
```

President Theodore Roosevelt was a popular and interesting president. He was an excellent athlete and enjoyed the outdoors. Learn more about his accomplishments. Circle the correct answer to complete the sentences.

1. Roosevelt believed in conservation and established (5/12) national parks during his presidency.

2. He was the first president to travel to a foreign country, (England/Panama), while in office.

3. He commanded the (Abolitionists/Rough Riders) in the Spanish-American War.

4. Roosevelt was the (youngest/oldest) man to become president.

5. He was the first American to win the (Nobel Peace Prize/Pulitzer Prize).

___ ___ ___ ___ ___ ___

___ ___ ___ ___ ___ ___ ___ ___

___ ___ ___ ___ ___ ___ ___

___ ___ ___ ___ ___ .

8

Scrambled Names

The names of 12 people from the 1900s have been split into two-letter segments. The letters of the segments are in order, but the segments are scrambled. Put the pieces together to identify the personality. (Clues are given in parenthesis.)

1. ET HS TA IZ AB EL NT ON (women's rights) _____

2. YR OO VE DD LT TE SE (president) _____

3. HI ND GA ND AS HA MO (world leader—India) _____

4. IN EI BE AL RT NS TE (scientist) _____

5. UN SI GM DF RE UD (psychologist) _____

6. DK RU AR DY IP NG LI (author) _____

7. AS BL PA OP IC SO (artist) _____

8. GE LL WI RO RS (performer) _____

9. AN JA RV NA IS (Mother's Day) _____

10. DR AN EW RN CA EG IE (philanthropist) _____

11. WI UR LB WR HT IG (inventor) _____

12. CY MA GO NT ME UD LU MO RY (author) _____

Scout Law

Robert Baden-Powell of Great Britain began the Boy Scout organization in 1907. One year later, an American businessman, William D. Boyce, was helped by a Boy Scout while traveling in England. He was so impressed by the boy's helpfulness, he brought the organization to the United States.

Boy Scouts take an oath in which they promise to do their duty. They also pledge to follow the Scout Law, which has 12 points. Those points are hidden in the puzzle below. The first four have been done for you. Fill in the eight missing words.

WORD BANK: loyal, helpful, thrifty, friendly, cheerful, reverent, trustworthy, clean

Australia

Australia became an independent nation on January 1, 1901. Fill in the blanks to complete the words. When read from top to bottom, the word made by the underlined letters will have something to do with Australia.

EXAMPLE:

```
R  O  P  E
M  U  S  T
S  T  E  P
A  B  L  E
C  A  S  T
A  C  H  E
S  K  I  P
```
(underlined letters: O U T B A C K)

1.
```
H O ___ E
D I ___ T
P A ___ N
D I ___ H
B O ___ K
S E ___ D
D E ___ P
T U ___ N
H O ___ T
```
the first white inhabitants

2.
```
C ___ N D Y
A ___ O U T
F ___ L D S
A ___ R O W
S ___ G N S
A ___ A I N
B ___ K E R
S ___ E A K
M ___ E T S
A ___ K E D
```
native Australians

3.
```
___ A R E
___ C H E
___ E C K
___ I R D
___ A C H
___ E A D
___ I N G
___ L S O
```
Australia's capital city

4.
```
B E ___ T
R A ___ E
S E ___ T
H A ___ S
N E ___ D
W E ___ T
```
Australia has six of these

5.
```
S ___ A R
G ___ O D
I ___ C H
S ___ O P
D ___ P S
O ___ L Y
T ___ S T
S ___ A P
S ___ A Y
```
Australia is a country and a ____.

6.
```
C A ___ I N
B A ___ N S
P A ___ N T
B I ___ E S
G R ___ I N
S H ___ P S
L E ___ D S
```
Australia was granted independence from _____.

7.
```
W I ___ G L E
P O ___ D L E
I S ___ A N D
S A ___ D L E
```
_____ was discovered in 1851.

8.
```
S T A R ___
R E A D ___
D A T E ___
G R E E ___
G L O B ___
P A R T ___
```
a large Australian city

#2601 20th Century Quiz Book

Australian Independence

The new nation of Australia was born on January 1, 1901. It is the sixth largest country in the world and the only one that is also a continent. It is sparsely populated with an average of only six people per square mile and a total population of about 20 million.

Most of the people live on the southeastern coast.

Australia has seven states:

1. Western Australia

2. Northern Territory

3. Queensland

4. South Australia

5. New South Wales

6. Victoria

7. Tasmania

The main cities are these:

1. Sydney

2. Melbourne

3. Perth

4. Canberra.

Label the map of Australia.

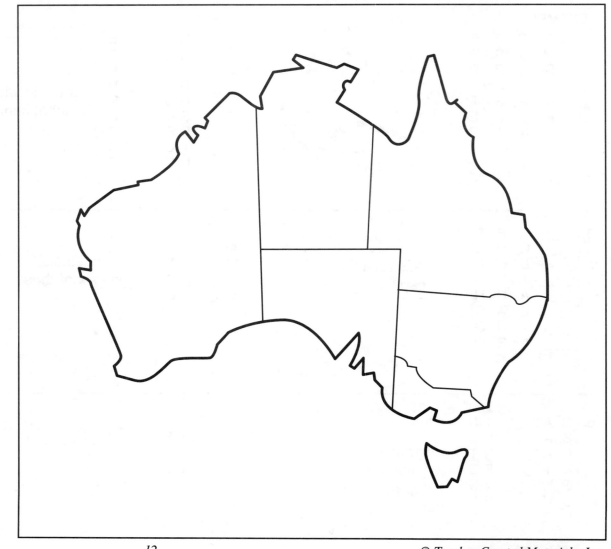

Three of a Kind

Below are various categories relating to the 1900s. List three or more people, places, or important dates associated with each category.

1. suffragettes _____

_____

2. Temperance Movement _____

_____

3. Nobel Prize winners _____

_____

4. sports _____

_____

5. artists _____

_____

6. writers _____

_____

7. world leaders _____

_____

8. athletes _____

_____

9. scientists _____

_____

10. inventions _____

_____

11. Industrial Revolution _____

_____

12. political revolutions and wars _____

_____

13. explorers _____

_____

14. presidential assassination _____

_____

Nobel Prize Winners

The Nobel Prize was created by Alfred Nobel, a Swedish chemist who invented dynamite. In his will, he left nine million dollars, the interest from which would be used for cash prizes in the categories of physics, chemistry, medicine, literature, and peace.

The first Nobel Prize was awarded in 1901. In 1969, a sixth prize category, economic science, was added by the Bank of Sweden.

Read these clues and then identify the winners.

1. This Polish trade union leader became president of his country. He won in 1983. _____

2. This Bishop of South Africa helped bring peace to his country. He won in 1984. _____

3. This U.S. president won in 1919 for his work with the League of Nations. _____

4. This former Canadian Secretary of State of External Affairs and United Nations president won in 1957. _____

5. This scientist discovered the photoelectric effect. He won in 1921. _____

6. This U.S. president won in 1906 for his part in the collaboration of several peace treaties. _____

7. This man won two prizes, in 1954 and 1962, for his work in chemistry and nuclear peace treaties. He also wrote the book *Vitamin C and the Common Cold.* _____

8. This woman won in 1979 for her work helping the poor people of India. _____

9. This woman won in 1911 for the discovery of radioactivity and studies of uranium. _____

10. This man won in 1904 for his work on the physiology of digestion. _____

11. This man won in 1964 for leading nonviolent civil rights demonstrations in the U.S. _____

12. This woman won in 1931 for her work with the Women's International League for Peace and Freedom. _____

13. This man won in 1907 for his stories, novels, and poems. _____

14. This man won in 1918 for stating the quantum theory of light. _____

15. This doctor won in 1952 for his humanitarian work in Africa. _____

16. This British prime minister won in 1953 for literature. _____

17. This Latin American woman won in 1945 for her contribution to literature and poetry. _____

Headlines

Use a reference book to help you find the people or places referred to in each of these headlines.

1. _____ Author's work, *The Wonderful Wizard of Oz,* Published (1900)

2. _____ Retiring Steel Baron Gives Away Fortune (1901)

3. _____ Indian Territory Given to Settlers (1901)

4. _____ President Shot: Assassin Arrested (1901)

5. _____ U.S. Pays $40 Million for Right to Dig in Central America (1902)

6. _____ President Helps Settle Coal Strike (1902)

7. _____ Stock Exchange Opens with Ticker Tape Parade (1903)

8. _____ Engineer Will Manufacture Horseless Carriage (1903)

9. _____ First World Series Won by American League Team (1903)

10. _____ President Inaugurated During Snowstorm (1909)

11. _____ Explorer Plants U.S. Flag on North Pole (1909)

12. _____ Apache Leader Dies at 80 (1909)

13. _____ Olympics Open in British Capital (1908)

14. _____ Nobel Prize Goes to Writer in India (1907)

15. _____ European Immigrants Continue to Enter U.S. (1907)

16. _____ U.S. Territory Rejects Statehood. (1906)

Word Bank

- Ellis Island
- London
- Robert Peary
- Boston
- New York City
- Panama
- Oklahoma Territory
- Lyman Frank Baum
- Andrew Carnegie
- William McKinley
- Theodore Roosevelt
- Henry Ford
- William Howard Taft
- Geronimo
- Rudyard Kipling
- Arizona

R.I.P.

Here are sayings, or epitaphs, that might have appeared on the tombstones of famous artists, writers, and musicians from the 1900s. Read the clues and fill in their names. Use a reference book to add the year each one died.

1. This person is best known for colorful depictions of entertainers in Paris.

   Here lies _____

   (1864 – _____)

2. This French Impressionist painter helped develop the style known as "synthetism."

   Here lies _____

   (1848 – _____)

3. This American painter is best known for a portrait of his mother.

   Here lies _____

   (1834 – _____)

4. This French sculptor designed the Statue of Liberty.

   Here lies _____

   (1834 – _____)

5. This French author wrote *Around the World in Eighty Days*.

   Here lies _____

   (1828 – _____)

6. This Norwegian poet and playwright is best remembered for his play *A Doll's House*.

   Here lies _____

   (1828 – _____)

7. This French Impressionist is best known for his landscape paintings.

   Here lies _____

   (1839 – _____)

8. This Russian composer who wrote *Scheherazade* was once a teacher of Igor Stravinsky.

   Here lies _____

   (1844 – _____)

9. This person is the American author of Uncle Remus stories.

   Here lies _____

   (1848 – _____)

10. This Czech composer's symphonies were inspired by American folk music themes.

    Here lies _____

    (1841 – _____)

Take Your Vitamins

In 1912, a British biochemist, Frederick Hopkins, proved that certain food substances were necessary for growth and development. He called these substances "accessory food factors." They were different from carbohydrates, fats, minerals, proteins, and water. A Polish biochemist, Casimir Funk, named these substances *vitamins*.

Since that time, 13 vitamins have been identified. Here is a list of vitamin-rich foods with information about how they help your body grow.

Vitamin A (helps maintain skin, eyes, bones, and teeth): carrots, dark leafy vegetables

Vitamin B1 (helps heart and nervous system function): nuts, meat, vegetables

Vitamin B2 (helps tissue repair and healthy skin): cheese, fish, milk

Vitamin B 12 (necessary for the development of red blood cells): fish, milk, meat

Vitamin C (builds sound bones and teeth): citrus fruits, tomatoes

Vitamin D (needed for calcium metabolism): eggs, tuna, salmon

Vitamin E (helps maintain cell membranes): almost all foods, including vegetable oils

Vitamin K (needed for normal blood clotting): leafy vegetables

Fill in the blanks with the "vitamin letters" A, B, C, D, E, and K to complete the story.

____ h____ ____lthy ____i____t h____s

m____ny ____iff____r____nt ____in____s of

foo____. You shoul____ ____ ____t fruits

____n____ v____g____t____ ____l____s,

____ ____r____ ____l ____n____

____r____ ____ ____, ____ ____ iry

pro____ucts, ____nd l ____ ____ n

m____ ____t ____v____ry ____ ____y.

____ ____ ____ ____r____ful not to

ov____r____ ____t foo____s high in

sug____r ____n____ f____t. ____ ____ting

th____ right foo____s will h____lp you

grow strong ____n____ h____ ____lthy.

Zipper King

The zipper was patented in 1913 by Gideon Sundback, a Swedish immigrant living in New Jersey. It was not used on everyday clothes for several years. In 1935 men's clothing manufacturers started replacing fly buttons with zippers. Today we use zippers in much of our clothing and other common items. Use the clues to complete this list of items that commonly have zippers.

B _ _ _ _ **G**

S _ **I** _ _ _ _ _

D _ _ _ _ **L**

T **E** _ _

S _ **O** _ _ _

S _ _ _ _ _ **N** _ B _ _

U _ _ _ _ **S** _ _ _ _ _

P **U** _ _ _

J _ _ **N** _

D _ _ _ S

B _ _ _ S

O _ _ _ **A** _ _ _

R _ _ _ **C** _ _ _

J _ _ **K** _ _

1. back pack
2. travel bag
3. gym bag
4. camper's home
5. summer pants
6. camper's bed

7. furniture covering
8. hand bag
9. denim pants
10. joined skirt and top
11. footwear
12. bibbed work clothes
13. waterproof outerwear
14. short coat

Father's Day

This holiday to honor fathers was first celebrated on June 19, 1910.

Read the clues and write the answers in the blanks. Then use the letters in the circles to answer the question.

1. day for traditional observance

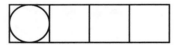

2. father's nickname

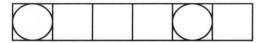

3. children's nickname

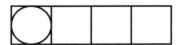

4. president who signed the holiday into law

5. holiday month

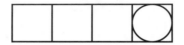

6. What was the U.S. city where Father's Day was first celebrated?

7. Rearrange the letters in these words to reveal the name of the founder of Father's Day.

RADIO   MELDS   DONUT   OR   AS   SO

__ __ __ __ __ __

__ __ __ __ __ __

__ __ __ __ __ __ __ __

Kindergarten

Margaretha Meyer Schurz began the kindergarten movement in the United States. Her schools for young children became popular during the second decade of the century. Use the clues to find these words made from the letters in **KINDERGARTEN**.

1. __ __ __ (color)

2. __ __ __ __ __ (color)

3. __ __ __ __ __ (number)

4. __ __ __ (number)

5. __ __ __ (finish)

6. __ __ __ __ __ (soil)

7. __ __ __ __ (precipitation)

8. __ __ __ __ __ (railroad)

9. __ __ __ __ __ (barter)

10. __ __ __ (beverage)

11. __ __ __ (fluid for writing)

12. __ __ __ __ (not light)

13. __ __ __ __ __ (cereal)

14. __ __ __ __ __ __ __
(evening meal)

15. __ __ __ __ __ __ __ __
(citrus fruit)

Picture Puzzle

Complete this challenging puzzle by cutting out the individual pieces to form a picture of an important symbol of the 1910s. Glue the completed puzzle onto colored construction paper. Who is the mystery person?

_____

person

Who Done It?

Solve these mysteries with names of famous people from the 1910s. Study the clues and then use a reference book to help find the answers.

1. *The Mona Lisa* (da Vinci masterpiece) was stolen from the Louvre in Paris. (1911)

   Who done it? _____

2. This Norwegian explorer was the first to reach the South Pole. (1911)

   Who done it? _____

3. This female scientist won her second Nobel Prize in 1911.

   Who done it? _____

4. This doctor eliminated yellow fever and malaria at the site of the building of the Panama Canal. (1913)

   Who done it? _____

5. Archduke Ferdinand and his wife were gunned down in the streets of Sarajevo. (1914)

   Who done it? _____

6. Former heavyweight fighter James J. Jeffries came out of retirement but was defeated by this boxer. (1910)

   Who done it? _____

7. The British liner *Lusitania* was sunk in 1915.

   Who done it? _____

8. Tsar Nicholas and his family were executed in 1918.

   Who done it? _____

9. Mata Hari was executed for espionage in 1917.

   Who done it? _____

10. This German physicist won the Nobel Prize for the quantum theory in 1918.

    Who done it? _____

11. This leader introduced postwar Italy to a new political organization.
    Who done it? _____

12. A peace treaty ending World War I was signed at Versailles, France, in 1919.

    Who done it? _____

13. An overworked U.S. president abandoned a national tour due to poor health in 1919.

    Who done it? _____

14. This Greek king abdicated the throne to avoid a provisional war government.

    Who done it? _____

15. Thousands of Armenians were murdered in Turkey. (1915)

    Who done it? _____

Labor Reform

Use the diagrams to decode these changes in early labor practices.

A	B	C
D	E	F
G	H	I

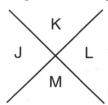

N•	O•	P•
Q•	R•	S•
T•	U•	V•

Example: ⌐⌐LV□⌐ <⌐•□ PICKET LINE

1. <⌐∧⌐⅂⌐⌐⌐ L⌐⌐<⌐ <⌐U⌐□
   _____

2. ⌐⌐U⌐⌐⌐⌐⌐⌐ V⌐□V ⌐⌐<
   _____

3. ⌐⌐⌐□□ V⌐□V⌐⌐⌐ L⌐⌐⌐⌐⌐⌐⌐⌐
   _____

4. ⌐⌐L□□⌐□□ V⌐⌐□⌐
   _____

5. L□□⌐⌐⌐⌐⌐ ⌐⌐ <⌐U⌐□ ⌐⌐⌐⌐⌐
   _____

6. V⌐□V□□ ⌐⌐⌐⌐V□⌐
   _____

7. ⌐⌐⌐⌐⌐⌐⌐⌐< □□⌐⌐<⌐⌐⌐⌐⌐
   _____

8. ∧⌐⌐ ⌐□□⌐⌐⌐⌐⌐⌐
   _____

9. >⌐□ ⌐□L⌐□⌐⌐<
   _____

10. ⌐□⌐⌐⌐⌐⌐ ⌐⌐⌐□
    _____

Slang Terms and Nicknames

Here are some new words that were invented during the 1910s. See if you can tell their meanings.

1. Someone who is influential

2. A comment intended to hurt someone's feelings

3. Something that is easy to do

4. A car trip taken just for fun

5. Slang term for bad or inferior

6. An individual lacking a high degree of cultural knowledge

7. Slang term for fine or excellent

8. A secret that is told unintentionally

9. To hold someone's interest without satisfying his desire

10. A factory or business with poor working conditions

11. U.S. World War I troops

Many of the important figures of the 1910s were known by nicknames. See if you can name these people.

12. Big Four _____

13. Manassas Mauler _____

14. Little Tramp _____

15. America's Sweetheart _____

16. Georgia Peach _____

17. Buffalo Bill _____

18. Red Baron _____

19. Lady of the Lamp _____

20. Rough Rider _____

Word Bank

- doughboys
- big shot
- cutting remark
- sweat shop
- it's a cinch
- joyride
- string along
- lousy
- spill the beans
- peachy
- lowbrow

Word Bank

- Theodore Roosevelt
- Lloyd George
- Florence Nightingale
- Jack Dempsey
- Charlie Chaplin
- Manfred von Richtofen
- Ty Cobb
- Mary Pickford
- William F. Cody
- Orlando
- Clemenceau
- Wilson

Panama Canal

In 1904, the United States gained the rights to build a canal through Panama. When the canal opened on August 15, 1914, it shortened the journey for ships navigating from the Pacific Ocean to the Atlantic Ocean from seven thousand miles to only forty miles. Use the clues to decode these words relating to the construction of the Panama Canal.

1. Location of Panama ☐☐☐☐☐☐ ☐☐☐☐☐☐☐

2. Jungle diseases that killed many workers ☐☐☐☐☐☐☐, ☐☐☐☐☐ ☐☐☐☐☐

3. First country to try to build the canal ☐☐☐☐☐☐

4. U.S. President who began the construction ☐☐☐☐☐☐☐ ☐☐☐☐☐☐☐☐☐

5. Type of canal construction ☐☐☐☐ ☐☐☐ ☐☐☐☐

6. Chief engineer on the project ☐☐☐☐☐☐ ☐☐☐☐☐☐

7. U.S. President who opened the canal ☐☐☐☐☐☐ ☐☐☐☐☐☐

8. Doctor who found a way to control the diseases (See question 2.) ☐☐☐☐☐☐ ☐☐☐☐☐☐

9. First ship to pass through the canal ☐☐☐☐☐

10. Fee charged to pass through the canal ☐☐☐☐

11. Term for ships from many different countries ☐☐☐☐☐☐☐☐☐☐☐☐

12. Narrow waterway ☐☐☐☐☐☐☐

13. Narrow strip of land ☐☐☐☐☐☐☐

14. Raised access road built across water ☐☐☐☐☐☐☐☐☐

15. Document giving Panama ownership of the canal in 2000 ☐☐☐☐☐☐ ☐☐☐☐☐ ☐☐☐☐☐☐

News of the Decade

See how well you remember the events of the 1910s. Circle the year in which each event occurred.

1. The Germans sink the British liner *SS Lusitania*.

   1915   **1920**   **1922**

2. The Russian Revolution comes to an end. Communists take over.

   1913   **1917**   **1922**

3. Henry Ford begins assembly-line techniques in production of Model T cars.

   1917   **1913**   **1910**

4. The "unsinkable" *Titanic* sinks.

   1910   **1911**   **1912**

5. World War I ends with Germany's defeat.

   1917   **1918**   **1919**

6. The Inca city Machu Picchu is discovered in Peru.

   1911   **1912**   **1914**

7. The Panama Canal opens, linking the Atlantic and Pacific Oceans.

   1914   **1915**   **1918**

8. The United States enters World War I.

   1912   **1915**   **1917**

9. Jim Thorpe becomes the first athlete to win Olympic medals in the pentathlon and the decathlon.

   1911   **1912**   **1913**

10. Women first competed in the summer Olympics in this year.

    1910   **1911**   **1912**

11. The first Father's Day was celebrated in June of this year.

    1910   **1911**   **1912**

12. George V is crowned King of the British Empire.

    1910   **1911**   **1912**

13. Marie Curie received a second Nobel Prize for the discovery of radium and polonium.

    1910   **1911**   **1912**

14. John F. Kennedy, 35th U.S. President, was born this year.

    1916   **1917**   **1918**

15. Pierre Elliot Trudeau, Canadian Prime Minister, was born this year.

    1917   **1918**   **1919**

Disaster on the High Seas

Analyze these groups of letters to solve the puzzles. They are in order, no letters have been omitted, but they cannot be read left to right. Patterns may be horizontal or vertical. Pay close attention to the clues provided.

1

J	B	L	E	T	U	S
D	N	A	T	I	M	N
L	I	C	X	Y	O	H

It was thought that this luxury liner could not sink.

2

Y	C	T	H	B	P	D
E	A	A	I	U	E	O
J	R	P	A	K	N	Z

This ship responded to the luxury liner's SOS.

3

E	I	L	A	C	F	N
Q	F	O	R	N	J	E
U	S	X	E	I	A	K

This ship did not receive the luxury liner's signal for help.

4

Y	O	Y	W	E	N	L
Z	R	K	C	I	T	Y
C	J	M	A	X	P	Q

The original destination of the luxury liner was for this American city.

5

X	B	E	E	G	A	E
L	E	C	R	N	I	K
M	R	I	O	A	G	M
O	G	S	U	D	Z	N

Hitting this caused the disaster.

6

R	C	W	A	I	W	G
P	A	D	R	T	A	H
Q	P	E	D	H	L	D
J	T	N	S	T	I	B
Z	A	I	M	I	K	O

This captain went down with his ship.

7

D	K	P	S	A	P	H
R	L	D	T	F	J	L
S	M	N	I	L	N	M
Z	W	A	R	E	O	C
T	A	L	E	B	U	D

The luxury liner was built in this city and country.

8

M	T	S	N	H	J	G
N	O	A	J	O	E	I
Y	R	B	A	J	U	Z
K	F	O	C	P	W	H

This American millionaire was a passenger who died on the ship.

Telegrams

Years before we had fax machines and e-mail, people sent urgent messages around the world over telegraph lines. Telegrams were sent in Morse code, received at a central office, printed on paper, and delivered by messengers. Fill in the words that complete the following telegrams. The word "stop" was used as a period because Morse code did not include punctuation.

1. 1910 "Edison invention revolutionizes entertainment industry *stop* Moviegoers enjoy

_____*stop*"

2. 1914 "First ship passes from Pacific to Atlantic *stop* Americans cheer opening of

_____*stop*"

3. 1915 "Passenger liner torpedoed killing 1,200 *stop* German sub sinks

_____*stop*"

4. 1917 "Tsar Nicholas II abdicates throne *stop* Revolutionaries install

_____as

new leader *stop* "

5. 1912 "Luxury liner hits iceberg *stop* 1,517 people lost in sinking of

_____*stop*"

6. 1912 "Native American athlete wins medals in pentathlon and decathlon at 1912

_____*stop*"

7. 1910 "Spokane woman's efforts successful *stop* June 10 will be first

_____*stop*"

8. 1918 "Influenza

_____*stop*

kills 20 million people worldwide *stop* Hospitals cannot handle numbers *stop*"

9. 1919 "Women's Christian Temperance Union campaigns against purchase and consumption of

_____ stop

Legislation pending *stop*"

10. 1917 "Women suffragettes take stand for_____*stop*"

11. 1919 "Paris Peace Conference opposes Wilson's Fourteen Points *stop*

_____

stop seems unlikely"

12. 1916 "Legislature passes Keating-Owen Act *stop* Federal ban on

_____*stop*"

The Great War

Fill in the blanks to complete the words. When read from top to bottom, the word made by the underlined letters will have something to do with World War I. The first one has been done for you.

1.
```
S  H  A  P  E
H  O  _  L  _  E  Y
D  R  _  L  _  A  D  _  Y  S
R  _  A  _  L  _  D  _  S  S
S  _  E  _  I  _  D  _  S  E
W  _  A  _  S  _  T  _  E
```

2.
```
S  _  O  P
L  _  O  N  _  L  I  D  Y  P
O  _  U  N  _  L  I  E  _  Y  P  D
S  _  U  _  L  I  E  _  D
U  _  _  E  D
```

3.
```
S  L  _  E  P
C  O  _  L  _  E  S  M
S  C  O  _  T  _  E  A  B  S  R
S  C  F  O  _  L  _  B  _  E  M  S  R
F  L  _  E  R
```

4.
```
U  _  H  E  R
Q  _  E  _  E  U
A  _  A  _  O  _  N  T
A  _  P  _  B  _  E  N  R  S
P  _  A  _  I  _  N  O  T  S  W
A  _  W  _  R  _  O  E  I  D  L
W  _  U  _  P  _  E  I  S
U  _  M  _  T  _  I  T  L
M  _  _  L  _  T  S
```

5.
```
S  T  _  N  D
F  A  _  _  M  D  S
T  O  _  B  _  S  S  E
M  A  _  B  _  E
```

6.
```
_  O  R  C  E
_  R  D  _  C  E  R  E  Y
_  A  N  _  G  E  R  Y
_  A  R  _  R  G  Y
_  V  E  R  Y
```

7.
```
R  E  _  O  V  E
C  H  _  R  _  M  O  S  E
M  I  _  R  _  N  Z  R  G
F  A  _  I  _  O  N  L  D
B  E  _  O  _  L  G  D
```

8.
```
T  H  A  _
A  S  R  E  A  _
S  B  H  T  R  U  A  G  _
B  H  R  U  I  A  G  O  _
R  I  O  _
```

9.
```
D  _  R  T  Y
U  _  D  _  E  R  Y
E  _  E  _  R  S  Y  E
T  _  S  _  O  T  R  E  S
O  _  O  _  V  R  E  N
S  _  V  _  E  N
```

10.
```
M  _  R  R  Y
S  _  A  _  H  R  Y  S
O  _  P  _  H  N  E  R  T  S  S
P  _  S  _  N  O  I  T  P  S  E
S  _  I  _  P  S
```

11.
```
_  R  I  L  L
_  V  E  R  _  L  Y
_  I  D  _  G  E  R  Y
_  O  G  _  V  R  E  Y  R
_  N  _  U  R  S  V  R  S
_  E  O  _  U  R  S
```

12.
```
B  U  L  _
G  A  L  L  _
D  O  L  _
W  A  L  L  _
M  A  M  _
K  I  L  L  _
M  I  S  _
```

A Tale of Two Presidents 1910–1919

From 1910 to 1919, two men had the honor and responsibility of leading the United States of America as president. They also shared the following letters in their names: D R W O L I. A list of their statements, activities, and accomplishments follows. Your challenge is to identify the presidents and write their names next to their activities, statements, and accomplishments.

Activities and Accomplishments	President
1. President of Princeton University	_____
2. Governor of the Philippines	_____
3. Governor of New Jersey	_____
4. Chief Justice of the U.S. Supreme Court	_____
5. Established the U.S. Postal System	_____
6. Vigorously prosecuted the Sherman Antitrust Law	_____
7. Served as U.S. Secretary of War	_____
8. Established the Federal Reserve Banking System	_____
9. Founded the League of Nations	_____
10. Promoted "Dollar Diplomacy"	_____
11. Elected president because "He kept us out of war"	_____
12. Opposed "Dollar Diplomacy"	_____
13. Asked Congress to declare war against Germany	_____
14. Established Federal Children's Bureau	_____
15. Established Parcel Post	_____

Cartoon Genius

In 1923, Walt Disney and his brother Roy formed a company. They began making cartoons. Some of their most popular characters include Mickey Mouse, Minnie Mouse, Pluto, Donald Duck, and Goofy. The brothers' company, Walt Disney Productions, later made cartoons into films like *Snow White and the Seven Dwarfs*, *Sleeping Beauty*, *Cinderella*, *Pinnochio*, and *Dumbo*. Disney's other accomplishments include television shows, live action movies, and theme parks.

Read the riddles and answer with the name of a popular cartoon character or film.

1. I starred in a cartoon called Steamboat Willie. My original name was Mortimer. Who am I?

   _____

2. I fell into a deep sleep after eating a poisoned apple. Who am I? _____

3. My coach turned into a pumpkin at midnight. Who am I? _____

4. My nose grew because I told a lie. Who am I? _____

5. I'm Mickey's girlfriend. Who am I? _____

6. I have webbed feet and three nephews. Who am I? _____

7. I'm Mickey's dog. Who am I? _____

8. I'm a dog who does everything backwards. Who am I? _____

9. They laughed at my big ears. Who am I? _____

10. I was awakened by the kiss of a handsome prince. Who am I? _____

Walt Disney

Food Chain

Diabetes is a disease which causes people to have difficulty metabolizing sugar properly. Diabetics must carefully manage the amount and types of food they eat. The disease can be very serious if left untreated. In 1922, Dr. Frederick Banting, a Canadian surgeon, studied the effects of insulin on the pancreas and developed a successful treatment for diabetes. Dr. Banting won the Nobel Prize in medicine for his work.

Use the letter clues to help you complete a chain of common foods. Notice the last letter of the first word becomes the first letter of the next word.

1. C __ __ __ __ L

2. L __ __ __ __ __ E

3. E __ __ S

4. S __ __ P

5. P __ __ __ __ T

6. T __ __ __ __ O

7. O __ __ __ N

8. N __ __ __ __ __ S

9. S __ __ __ __ __ H

10. H __ __ __ __ __ __ __ R

11. R __ __ __ __ __ S

12. S __ __ __ __ __ E

Challenge: Can you add three more words to the food chain?

I've Got Your Number

Use what you know about the 1920s to answer each question with a number.

1. Which amendment gave women the right to vote? _____

2. Which amendment prohibited the consumption of alcohol? _____

3. How many Academy Awards were won by Walt Disney? _____

4. How many home runs were hit by Babe Ruth in his best season? _____

5. At what age did Charles Lindbergh fly solo across the Atlantic Ocean? _____

6. How many U.S. Presidents are pictured on Mount Rushmore? _____

7. How many Olympic gold medals were won by Sonja Henie? _____

8. How many years were needed for Stalin's economic plan for Russia? _____

9. How many days did it take for Nelly Bly to travel around the world? _____

10. What was the price of a candy bar in 1920? _____

11. At what age did Egypt's King Tutankhamen die? _____

12. At what age did Russia's Lenin die? _____

13. How many characters are in the Winnie-the-Pooh series? _____

14. What was the price of a loaf of bread in 1920? _____

15. How many states are in Australia? _____

Babe Ruth

Charles Lindbergh

King Tut Mask

Egyptian Excavations

Use the diagrams to decode the following terms.

A	B	C
D	E	F
G	H	I

N•	O•	P•
Q•	R•	S•
T•	U•	V•

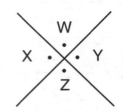

Example:

sarcophagus

1.

2.

3.

4.

5.

6.

7.

8.

9.

10.

11.

Product Slogans

Many of the products introduced in the 1920s are still popular today. Match these slogans to the products they might have advertised. Use the pictures as clues for some of the products.

1. It's faster than buttons, and it won't fall off!

_____

2. For a clean, fresh taste, try this chewing sensation.

_____

3. This will protect your small cuts from dirt and germs.

_____

4. These new, disposable handkerchiefs are convenient and inexpensive.

_____

5. This product will stick to paper instantly—no more waiting for messy glue.

_____

6. Try America's newest way to eat spuds!

_____

7. Fresher than canned foods—they go right from the freezer into your recipes.

_____

8. Imagine yourself in a new, curly "do."

_____

9. Try this new chocolate-covered ice cream on a stick.

_____

10. This tasty fruit spread is perfect on your morning toast.

_____

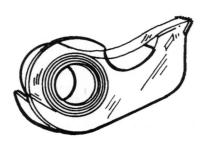     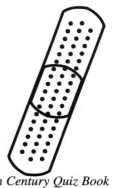

Words Within Words Within Words

Search these terms for small words, some of which may overlap. Write the words in the blanks.

1. ROARING TWENTIES

__ __ __ __ __ __ __

__ __ __ __ __ __

2. RED SCARE

__ __ __ __ __ __

3. TEAPOT DOME SCANDAL

__ __ __ __ __ __ __ __

__ __ __ __ __ __

__ __ __ __ __ __

4. SUFFRAGETTES

__ __ __ __ __

__ __ __

5. BROADCAST

__ __ __ __ __ __

6. DINETTE

__ __ __ __ __

__ __ __

7. TUTANKHAMEN

__ __ __ __ __ __ __

__ __ __ __ __ __

__ __ __ __

8. ANTARCTICA

__ __ __ __ __ __

__ __ __ __ __ __

9. INDUSTRY

__ __ __ __ __

__ __ __ __

10. PRESIDENT

__ __ __ __ __ __

__ __ __ __ __

__ __ __

Aussie Speak

When you think of Australia, you probably associate it with Paul Hogan, Mel Gibson, or Olivia Newton-John. In 1927, when Canberra became the federal capital of Australia, those names were not household words.

People in the "land down under" use special words to express many of their ideas. Many of their terms are descriptive and humorous and can be traced back to their English heritage. Here are some sentences in "Aussie speak." See if you can understand their meanings by substituting words from the word bank for the words in parentheses.

1. The (slacker) lost his job as town (garbo).

2. His (missus) had no (dough) to buy (tucker) for the (mob).

3. Three (ankle biters) (wagged) (kindy) because they were sick.

4. The family was driving out of town when their (donk) ran out of (petrol).

5. (Boomers) bounce around the (outback).

6. The (sheila) had an (ace) idea for killing a (Joe Blake).

7. (Ankle biters) like eating (lollies) and (water biscuits) with their (mates).

8. The old (bloke) went to the (chemist's) to buy medicine.

9. The poor (bloke) left his (brolley) and (torch) on the train.

10. Our (mob) uses a (lift) to reach our third floor apartment.

Word Bank

- friends
- candy
- lazy person
- garbage collector
- wife
- crackers
- money
- food

- umbrella
- elevator
- children
- skipped school
- kindergarten
- flashlight
- car engine
- gasoline

- kangaroos
- wilderness
- woman
- excellent
- snake
- man
- drugstore
- family

Create-a-Word Social Issues

Choose a part of a word from each column to form a new word about social issues in the twenties. Each part may be used only once. The first part of each word is in Column A. Write the new words in the blanks.

1. _____

2. _____

3. _____

4. _____

5. _____

6. _____

7. _____

8. _____

9. _____

10. _____

11. _____

12. _____

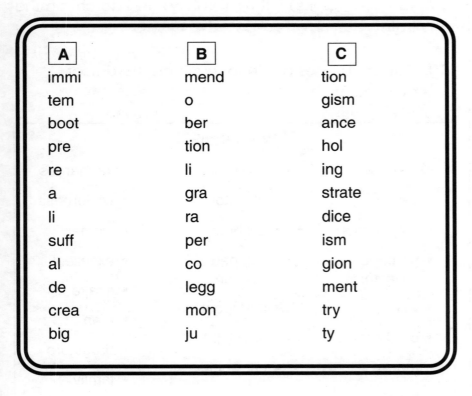

A	B	C
immi	mend	tion
tem	o	gism
boot	ber	ance
pre	tion	hol
re	li	ing
a	gra	strate
li	ra	dice
suff	per	ism
al	co	gion
de	legg	ment
crea	mon	try
big	ju	ty

38

Three Clues

Write the name of a famous person for each set of clues. *There are more names listed in the word bank than are needed.*

1. Red Sox, home run hitter, Yankees _____

2. 1919 World Series, indictment, gambling _____

3. 29th president, Republican, normalcy _____

4. murderers, Italians, guilty _____

5. Egypt, tomb, archaeology _____

6. Russian Revolution, Bolshevik, Gorky _____

7. Tennessee, evolution, biology teacher _____

8. magician, escape artist, water torture _____

9. New York, Paris, solo flight _____

10. Cotton Club, Big Band, piano music _____

11. flight, Atlantic Ocean, first woman _____

12. emperor, Japan, world peace _____

13. French, fashion designer, simplicity _____

14. explorer, Antarctica, polar flight _____

15. bacteriologist, penicillin, bread mold _____

Word Bank

- Babe Ruth
- Alexander Fleming
- "Shoeless" Joe Jackson
- Commander Richard Byrd
- Warren G. Harding
- Coco Chanel
- Sacco and Vanzetti
- Emperor Hirohito
- Tutankhamen
- Amelia Earhart
- Vladimir Lenin
- Duke Ellington
- Charles Lindbergh
- John Scopes
- Harry Houdini
- Benito Mussolini
- William Jennings Bryan
- Satchel Paige
- Langston Hughes
- Charlie Chaplin

Charles Lindbergh

Satchel Paige

Babe Ruth

The Twenties

On the diagram to the right, cross out the answers to the following questions.

1. A gangster who made millions of dollars selling illegal alcohol

2. The 18th Amendment which made it illegal to buy, sell, or drink alcohol

3. Women who wore short hair, short skirts, and makeup

4. Music popularized by African Americans in Harlem

5. Group that beat and murdered innocent African Americans

6. Date of the stock market crash

7. Clubs that served illegal alcohol

8. Sports heroes

9. The first automobile made on an assembly line.

10. Movie stars

11. Famous women

12. Inventions

13. U.S. presidents

14. Women who founded Planned Parenthood

15. Attorneys at the Scopes Trial

The remaining words are a common nickname given the decade.

It was called the _____ _____

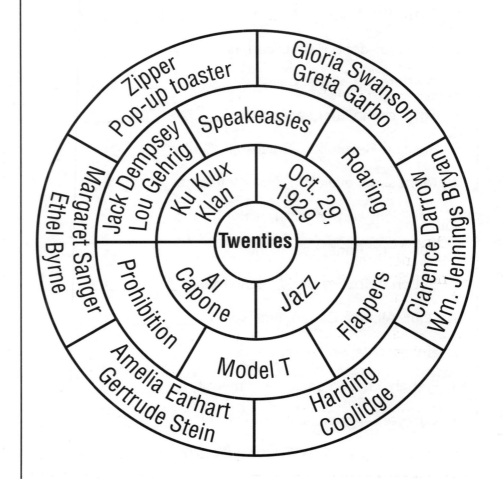

Sound and Silence

Motion pictures (or the "movies") achieved great popularity in the 1920s. It was this decade that saw the advent of sound in motion pictures, first called "talkies." In 1926, Warner Brothers Studio introduced the first really practical sound films using the process called Vitaphone. Some of the great figures of early silent films successfully made the shift to sound, but some did not. To the right is a list of memorable figures who achieved fame in those transitional years, along with some famous film titles associated with them. See if you can match the person with the film and identify the movie as silent or sound.

Person	Film	Sound or Silent
_____1. Al Jolson	A. *Our Hearts Were Young and Gay*	_____
_____2. Walt Disney	B. *Nanook of the North*	_____
_____3. Charlie Chaplin	C. *Steamboat Willie*	_____
_____4. Dorothy Gish	D. *The Iron Horse*	_____
_____5. Douglas Fairbanks	E. *The Sheik*	_____
_____6. Lillian Gish	F. *The Gold Rush*	_____
_____7. Buster Keaton	G. *The Freshman*	_____
_____8. Harold Lloyd	H. *The Mark of Zorro*	_____
_____9. Mary Pickford	I. *The Jazz Singer*	_____
_____10. Rudolph Valentino	J. *The Birth of a Nation*	_____
_____11. John Ford	K. *Sherlock, Jr.*	_____
_____12. Robert Flaherty	L. *Coquette*	

Headlines

Identify the people mentioned in these news articles.

1. President's Plan Leads to Stock Market Crash _____

2. Sultan of Swat Hits 60th Home Run _____

3. Physicist Wins Nobel Prize for Theories on Light _____

4. First Female Pilot Receives License _____

5. 15-Year-Old Wins Olympic Skating Gold _____

6. Library Created for Black Culture Collection _____

7. Teacher Convicted in Monkey Trial _____

8. "Little Tramp" Stars in Silent Movie _____

9. *Spirit of St. Louis* Lands Safely in Paris _____

10. Manufacturer Revolutionizes Auto Industry _____

11. Sculptor Begins Mount Rushmore Project _____

12. South American Writer Wins Nobel Prize _____

13. Tutankhamen's Tomb Opened in Egypt _____

14. American Pilot Flies Over South Pole _____

15. Painter's Cubism Shocks the World _____

Follow the Yellow Brick Road

The Wizard of Oz is one of the most watched movies of all time. It is the story of a girl who is swept away to the magical land of Oz where she meets a scarecrow, a tin man, and a cowardly lion. It was first shown on television in 1956. See what you can remember about this famous children's movie.

1. Who wrote the book that was made into the movie? _____

2. What Hollywood studio made the movie? _____

3. Who played the role of Dorothy? _____

4. What was the name of Dorothy's dog? _____

5. In what state did Dorothy live? _____

6. What weather condition carried her to the Land of Oz? _____

7. What did the tin man need? _____

8. What did the scarecrow need? _____

9. What did the cowardly lion need? _____

10. Name the most popular song from the movie. _____

Bonus:

What other famous American movie debuted in 1939? _____

Double Letters

Answer each clue with a word that contains double letters.

1. economic crash _____

2. favorite fruit _____

3. high number _____

4. 32nd U.S. president _____

5. communist country _____

6. Hitler's title _____

7. nickname for the Loch Ness monster

_____

8. first name of Berlin Olympic track star

_____

9. fairy tale brothers _____

10. forest home of Robin Hood _____

11. style of popular music _____

12. last word in the title of our national anthem

_____

13. 31st U.S. president _____

14. Dust Bowl state _____

15. Chicago community center _____

16. Grandma Moses' first name _____

17. "King of Swing" **(double double)**

_____

18. big band leader **(double double)**

_____

44

A Great Educator

Mary McLeod Bethune was the daughter of sharecroppers. She learned how to read and write during a time when there were no schools for African American children. After graduation from college, she opened her own school. Starting with the letter "E," write every third letter printed around the picture. The result will be the motto for Mrs. Bethune's original school.

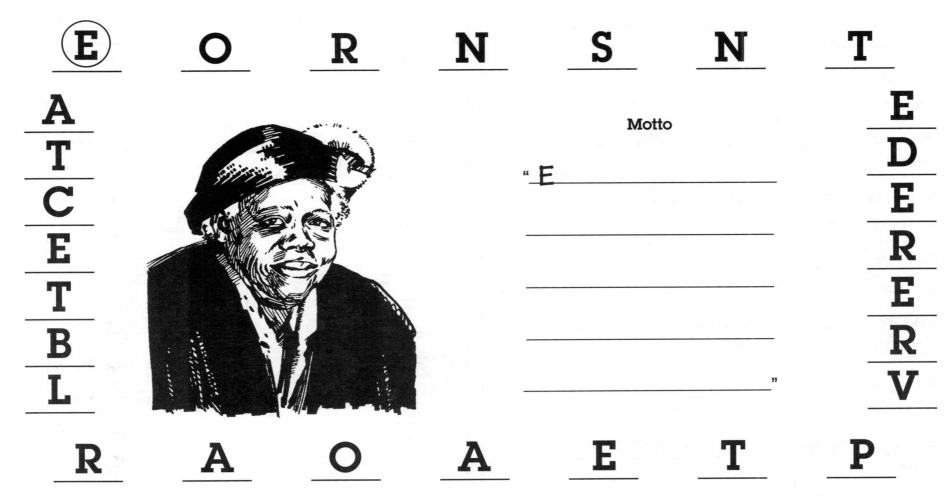

Motto

" E _____

_____

_____

_____

_____ "

Star-Spangled Banner

The words to the "Star-Spangled Banner" were written in 1814 by Francis Scott Key as he watched the bombardment of Fort McHenry. They were set to the tune of an English drinking song. On March 3, 1931, President Herbert Hoover signed a bill that made the song the national anthem of the United States. Can you fill in the missing words in the first verse of the "Star-Spangled Banner"?

Oh, say can you _____, by the _____ early light,

What so proudly we _____ at the _____ last gleaming.

Whose broad _____ and bright _____, through the _____ fight,

O'er the _____ we watched were so gallantly _____?

And the _____ red glare, the _____ bursting in air,

Gave _____ through the night that our _____ was still there.

Oh say, does that _____ spangled banner yet wave

O'er the _____ of the free and the _____ of the brave?

Use a reference book to identify the years for these former United States flags.

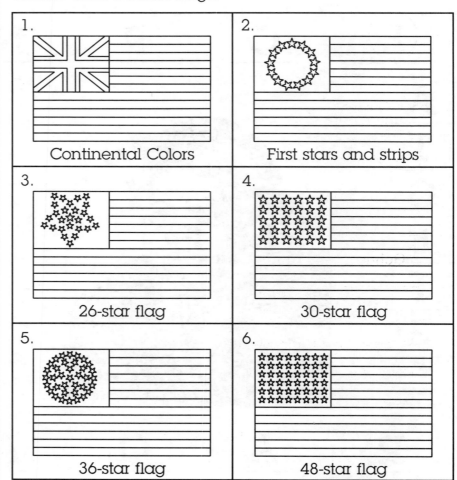

1. Continental Colors

2. First stars and strips

3. 26-star flag

4. 30-star flag

5. 36-star flag

6. 48-star flag

46

Athletes

A number of record-setting sports events occurred during the 1930s. There were many talented athletes. Use the clues to match the sport to the athlete. Mark the correct box with an X. One special athlete will have an X in two boxes.

Athlete	Figure Skating	Track and Field	Tennis	Golf	Boxing	Baseball
Sonja Henie						
Mildred "Babe" Didrikson Zaharias						
Jesse Owens						
Helen Wills Moody						
Joe Louis						
Lou Gehrig						

1. When I was 15, I competed in a knee-length skirt and white boots. _____

2. Besides the Olympics, I also played at Centre Court at Wimbledon. _____

3. Hitler disapproved of my athletic prowess. _____

4. I defended my title 25 times without a loss. _____

5. I was known as "The Iron Horse" because I played 2,130 games in a row. _____

6. In 1950, the Associated Press named me "The Greatest Woman Athlete." _____

Supermarket Shopping

The first supermarket opened in Queens, New York, in 1930. Wonder Bread sliced bread, Eggo frozen waffles, and Spam canned luncheon meat were new grocery items available to shoppers throughout the decade. Here are some incomplete shopping lists. Read the clues and fill in the answers.

Some foods go together naturally. Complete these combos.

1. potatoes and _____

2. fish and _____

3. cake and _____

4. soup and _____

5. peas and _____

6. meat and _____

7. peanut butter and _____

8. beans and _____

9. lettuce and _____

10. chips and _____

11. ham and _____

12. bread and _____

Some common foods are described with two names that begin with the same letter.

13. baked _____

14. cold _____

15. French _____

16. pepperoni _____

17. pumpkin _____

18. cheddar _____

19. strip _____

20. crispy _____

21. candy _____

22. frosted _____

23. rump _____

24. green _____

25. canned _____

26. spaghetti _____

27. black _____

Olympic Competitions

Fill in the missing letters to reveal information and highlights of the Olympics in 1932 and 1936.

_____ R O A D   J U M P

H A M M _____ R   T H R O W

M A _____ A T H O N

L U T Z _____ O N G

H _____ T L E R

_____ A Z I S

J E S S E _____ W E N S

B L A C K   A T H _____ E T E S

V I C T O R _____

G O L D _____ E D A L S

H I G H   J U M _____

A M E R _____ C A N S

D E _____ A T H L O N

T R A C K _____ T A R

P E N T A T H _____ O N

S H _____ T P U T

D I _____ C U S

T R _____ C K

B O X I _____ G

R O W I N _____

R _____ L A Y   R A C E S

W A T E R   P O _____ O

H U R D L _____ S

_____ W I M M I N G

L O N G   J U _____ P

F _____ N C I N G

_____ I V I N G

D E C _____ T H L O N

W R E S T _____ I N G

B A C K _____ T R O K E

What words are spelled by the letters in the blanks?

_____   _____

What words are spelled by the letters in the blanks?

_____   _____

Words Within Words

Use the clues to help you fill in the blanks with a small word. The answers relate to the politics and economics of the 1930s. *Clues are given in parentheses.*

1. G R E ___ ___   D E ___ ___ ___ ___ ___ I O N
    (*economy*)

2. L A B ___ ___   U N I ___ ___ S (*economy*)

3. P R O H I ___ ___ ___ I O N (*21st Amendment*)

4. M I G ___ ___ ___ I O N (*Dust Bowl*)

5. ___ ___ L I ___ ___ ___ T E R (*new aircraft*)

6. H O O V E R V ___ ___ ___ E S (*shanty towns*)

7. U N ___ ___ ___ ___ ___ ___ M E N T (*economy*)

8. P ___ ___ ___ ___ ___ ___ N T (*U.S. leader*)

9. ___ ___ C I A L   S E C U R ___ ___ Y (*New Deal*)

10. A ___ ___ L F   ___ ___ ___ L E R (*German leader*)

50

Quotes in Codes

Decode these presidential quotes.

Code	A	B	C	D	E	F	G	H	I	J	K	L	M	N	O	P	Q	R	S	T	U	V	W	X	Y	Z
Key	Y	Z	A	B	C	D	E	F	G	H	I	J	K	L	M	N	O	P	Q	R	S	T	U	V	W	X

1. "C ejkemgp kp gxgta rqv, c ect kp gxgta ictcig."
    —*Herbert Hoover*

" _____ ,

_____ . "

Code	A	B	C	D	E	F	G	H	I	J	K	L	M	N	O	P	Q	R	S	T	U	V	W	X	Y	Z
Key	Z	A	B	C	D	E	F	G	H	I	J	K	L	M	N	O	P	Q	R	S	T	U	V	W	X	Y

Herbert Hoover

2. "Uif pomz uijoh xf ibwf up gfbs jt gfbs jutfmg."
    —*Franklin Roosevelt*

" _____

_____ . "

Code	A	B	C	D	E	F	G	H	I	J	K	L	M	N	O	P	Q	R	S	T	U	V	W	X	Y	Z
Key	B	C	D	E	F	G	H	I	J	K	L	M	N	O	P	Q	R	S	T	U	V	W	X	Y	Z	A

3. "Ntq fqdzsdrs oqhlzqx szrj hr sn ots odnokd sn vnqj."
    —*Franklin Roosevelt*

Franklin Roosevelt

" _____

_____ . "

Creations of the Thirties

Use the telephone button diagram to help crack the code. Find each number on the telephone and use the dot to indicate the position of the letter which appears above it. See example.

A= •2

B= $\overset{\bullet}{2}$

C= 2•

(for the two letters not on the telephone, Z=0 and Q=1)

•8 6• 9• 7• | •2 $\overset{\bullet}{6}$ •3 | •4 •2 •6 $\overset{\bullet}{3}$ 7•

<u>toys</u>   <u>and</u>   <u>games</u>

1. •6 6• $\overset{\bullet}{6}$ 6• •7 6• 5• 9• _____

2. 9• 6• 9• 6• _____

3. $\overset{\bullet}{7}$ 6• 5• 5• $\overset{\bullet}{3}$ 7   7• $\overset{\bullet}{5}$ •2 •8 $\overset{\bullet}{3}$ 7•

_____   _____

4. •5 $\overset{\bullet}{8}$ •6 •7 $\overset{\bullet}{7}$ 6• •7 $\overset{\bullet}{3}$ _____

5. 3• $\overset{\bullet}{7}$ 6• 0 $\overset{\bullet}{3}$ $\overset{\bullet}{6}$ 3• 6• 6• •3

_____   _____

6. 7• •7 •2 •6 _____

7. •9 6• $\overset{\bullet}{6}$ •3 $\overset{\bullet}{3}$ 7 $\overset{\bullet}{2}$ $\overset{\bullet}{7}$ $\overset{\bullet}{3}$ •2 •3

8. 7• $\overset{\bullet}{6}$ 6• •9   •9 $\overset{\bullet}{4}$ 4• •8 $\overset{\bullet}{3}$ •2 $\overset{\bullet}{6}$ •3   •8 $\overset{\bullet}{4}$ $\overset{\bullet}{3}$

7• $\overset{\bullet}{3}$ 8• $\overset{\bullet}{3}$ $\overset{\bullet}{6}$ •3 •9 •2 $\overset{\bullet}{7}$ 3• 7•

_____   _____   _____

_____   _____

9. •8 $\overset{\bullet}{3}$ 5• $\overset{\bullet}{3}$ 8• 4• 7• 4• 6• $\overset{\bullet}{6}$ _____

10. 7• $\overset{\bullet}{8}$ •7 $\overset{\bullet}{3}$ $\overset{\bullet}{7}$ •6 •2 $\overset{\bullet}{6}$ _____

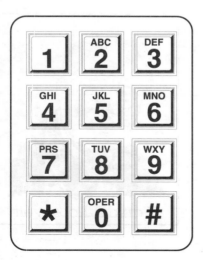

Trivia

Find the names of famous personalities from the 1930s.

1. This first couple sometimes spoke Chinese to assure having private conversations.

_____

2. Which presidential couple had four children in their first five years of marriage?

_____

3. Who was the first woman in the United States to earn a college degree in geology?

_____

4. Which scientist developed products from peanuts, sweet potatoes, and pecans?

_____

5. Who was the first woman to win the Nobel Peace Prize?

_____

6. This child star entered politics as an adult.

_____

7. This singer/songwriter created a style called "talking blues."

_____

8. Which track and field athlete was the first to go over the high bar headfirst?

_____

9. This composer of *Peter and the Wolf* died on the same day as Josef Stalin.

_____

10. Which writer who won both the Pulitzer and Nobel Prizes once worked as a maintenance man?

_____

11. Who was the only king of England ever to abdicate the throne?

_____

12. This mild-mannered superhero was first introduced in 1930s comic books.

_____

Analogies

To complete an analogy, you must first determine the relationship between the given items. The relationship may be person to birthplace, place to event, inventor to invention, etc. They are read as follows:

Igor Sikorsky:helicopter::Sir Frank Whittle:jet engine

(Igor Sikorsky is to the helicopter as Sir Frank Whittle is to the jet engine)

1. Herbert Hoover:Stanford::Franklin Roosevelt:
_____

2. Civilian Conservation Corps:parks::Public Works Administration:_____

3. Al Capone:_____::John Dillinger:
bank robber

4. dust bowl:farmers::stock market
crash:_____

5. Pearl Buck:*The Good Earth*::
_____:*Gone with the Wind*

6. Joe Louis:boxing::Jesse Owens:
_____

7. _____:Benny
Goodman::trombone:Glenn Miller

8. *American Gothic*:painting::*This Land Is Your
Land*:_____

9. _____:five offspring::twins:two
offspring

10. Adolf Hitler:_____::Chiang
Kai-shek:China

11. Clark Gable:actor::Greta Garbo:
_____

12. mobiles:_____::painting:Thomas Hart
Benton

13. Urban League:Mary McLeod Bethune::
_____:Marian Anderson

14. Great Depression:Herbert Hoover::New Deal:
_____

15. Romeo:Juliet::Edward VIII:_____

Picture Memory

Study the picture for three minutes. Then put it out of sight. On another sheet of paper, list as many items from the picture as you can remember.

Curious George

Hans and Margaret Rey came to the United States from Germany in 1940. They created Curious George, a monkey who is the leading character in a series of popular children's books. Here are some trivia questions about the original *Curious George* book.

1. What is George's favorite food?_____

2. What color was the man's hat? _____

3. Where did the man want to take George?

_____

4. What birds did George see on the deck of the ship?

_____

5. Who pulled George out of the water?

_____

6. Who came to the man's house when George played with the telephone? _____

7. Where did the firemen take George?

_____

8. How did George escape from prison?

_____

9. What was George holding when he flew into the air? _____

10. What color is the car of the man in the yellow hat?

_____

11. What was on the floor of George's prison cell?

_____

12. What animal was on the roof of the prison?

_____

13. How many children were with the balloon man?

_____

14. On what book did George sit while eating at the man's table? _____

15. What was on the floor at the foot of George's bed?

_____

Harry S Truman

Circle every third letter in the puzzle below to reveal the statement that explains Truman's feeling about his responsibility as president of the United States. Write the message below.

(T) G Y H V I E I
P B U R U V F C
I N K O M S R E
T P O O Y B P V
C S I K H T F E
P U R M G E A S

_ _ _ _ _ _

_ _ _ _ _ _ _

Harry S Truman was the first and only United States president to order an atomic bomb be dropped on another country. Write the correct answer to complete the sentences.

1. The atomic bomb was dropped on (Japan, Vietnam).

   _____

2. The bomb was dropped in (1954, 1945).

   _____

3. The cities that were bombed were (Hiroshima and Nagasaki, Tokyo and Hanoi).

   _____

4. The B-29 that dropped the bomb was called (*Amanda Ray, Enola Gay*)

   _____

5. The (Potsdam Treaty, Treaty of Tokyo) ended the war.

   _____

Made in the U.S.A.

The following products were being made in the U.S.A. during the 1940s. Find the products in the puzzle box to the right. The trick to solving the puzzle is that the words can be found in any direction. None of them are in a straight line. One has been done for you as an example.

Products

- computer
- transistor
- Slinky
- electric blanket
- Jeep
- M&Ms
- Silly Putty
- aerosol can
- Polaroid camera
- penicillin
- Elmer's Glue
- Morton Salt

```
J N P E Q K T R M Y W I C P Q & M F A J N I Q
P S T L I U S X O S T L A N G W K P E R O S T
E A L B E C T V D E B R U K J M I B U W X O K
N I G U A O U R I C & J G H E T O G N A C L A
P K C I L L G F X I D A F A O Y U K R H I D R
W X A T S I D H E O U C N I & L X A S W E J A
H M L E H N A F & M M O V W Z V C P J Z E P B
I N & T Y G I V T U P C U N I M U T T G F D C
P S M J N A P I E R K A B S L Y P A Y K I A M
Q X W I L U E M K U L T X O L L U B I L U R O
R Q E S G Q R & J L O P R U Z M Q R O N O T E
E L M R J Z K M Q A S W I V S A N S & S P J Z
I B E B U O Y C G R T R A & T R C I H I A R P
W X Q U L X K T S W O I D X B P D S T N C L S
L Z Y S L I N U N X M A C W A K M F O P E F T
& F E P J B K F A R E G H Z Y L R D R E K J Z
```

That's Entertainment!

Fill in the missing letters to reveal information about entertainment in the 1940s. The last one is filled in for you.

JITTER _____ UG

GLENN M _____ LLER

SWIN _____

_____ E-BOP

J _____ ZZ

FRANK SI _____ ATRA

AN _____ REW SISTERS

_____ USICALS

D _____ KE ELLINGTON

BOBBY _____ OXERS

D _____ ZZY GILLESPIE

BING _____ ROSBY

What words are spelled by the letters in the blanks?

_____

_____

_____

COS _____ UMES

C _____ OREOGRAPHY

CITIZ _____ N KANE

BRO _____ DWAY

DIREC _____ OR

G _____ NE KELLY

O _R_ SON WELLES

What word is spelled by the letters in the blanks?

_____

*Orson
Welles*

Read All About It

Use a reference book to help you fill in the date for each of these events.

1. _____ **Pearl Harbor Bombed FDR Declares War on Japan**

2. _____ FDR Inaugurated to 4th Term

3. _____ Men 21–36 Must Register for Draft

4. _____ U.S. Troops Land at Iwo Jima

5. _____ **FDR Dies—Truman Takes Oath**

6. _____ Winston Churchill Becomes Britain's Prime Minister

7. _____ Allies Invade Western Europe on D-Day

8. _____ Soviet Forces Free Jews at Auschwitz

9. _____ **Hitler Commits Suicide in Berlin**

10. _____ U.S. Drops 2nd A-Bomb—Japan Surrenders

60

Men and Women of WW II

World War II affected everyone in the country. Many men went to war, and most of the women who stayed at home worked behind the scenes to support the war effort. Read these clues to determine the contributions of these men and women.

	Pearl Harbor	Normandy France	Germany	Southern Italy	Sailor	Sergeant	Lieu-tenant	General
John								
James								
Thomas								
Edward								

	Red Cross	Airplane Factory	USO (United Service Organization)	Home	Bank
Rosie					
Clara					
Harriet					
Betty					
Sarah					

- "My ship was bombed by the Japanese on November 11, 1941."
- "I led a group of Allied privates into Sicily in July, 1943."
- "I commanded a tank in the Rhine Valley."
- "I led troops in a major attack that ended the war."

- Betty and Clara did volunteer work in the evenings. Clara is a nurse; Betty enjoys dancing.
- Rosie filled a "man's job."
- Harriet raised her children and enjoyed gardening.
- Sarah kept her job and bought war bonds with her extra money.

World War II Lists

The events, items, and people listed here were all significant to the war effort around the world. Read each list and fill in the titles.

1. _____

United States   England
Russia   Churchill
Eisenhower

2. _____

Germany   Italy
Japan   Tojo
Eichmann

3. _____

fat man   little boy
Nagasaki   Hiroshima
nuclear fallout

4. _____

Rosie the Riveter   rationing
victory garden   war bonds
selective service

5. _____

meat   sugar
butter   coffee
gasoline

6. _____

Dwight Eisenhower   Douglas MacArthur
George Patton   Omar Bradley
Ernie Pyle

7. _____

Hideki Tojo   Joseph Stalin
Benito Mussolini   Adolf Hitler
Winston Churchill

8. _____

spitfire   B-17
Stuka   B-29
Messerschmitt

9. _____

Dunkirk   D-Day
Pearl Harbor   Battle of the Bulge
Kursk

10. _____

concentration camps   "Jewish problem"
prisoners   ovens
six million killed

World War II

Analyze these groups of letters to solve the puzzles. They are in order, no letters have been omitted, but they cannot be read left to right. Patterns may be horizontal or vertical. Pay close attention to the clues provided.

```
C  X  Y  Z  B  J  G
P  A  R  B  O  H  E
M  E  L  R  R  I  A
O  P  H  A  X  D  K
```

Bombed by Japan

```
N  P  U  O  I  Z  Y
C  O  O  N  T  N  I
L  N  C  I  A  U  R
F  S  G  N  R  O  S
```

Supply and demand

```
X  S  O  R  I  B  A
Y  I  E  T  U  N  U
L  R  E  H  E  Q  K
J  I  V  E  A  T  G
S  R  E  T  U  V  W
```

Symbolized working women

```
Q  W  I  N  S  J  N
R  C  N  O  T  A  I
S  H  U  R  C  U  L
F  L  L  I  H  Z  X
```

British leader

```
Q  F  N  R  L  T  E
Z  R  I  O  E  A  O
J  A  L  O  V  G  U
M  N  K  S  E  N  D
```

American leader

```
B  X  A  M  T  J  Y
D  I  S  P  O  X  W
C  S  R  E  W  A  E
A  T  U  Q  Y  Z  X
```

Germany, Japan, and Italy formed this alliance

```
Z  U  O  D  J  A  Y
H  G  L  A  S  M  L
I  T  R  A  C  A  K
B  H  U  R  K  T  G
```

Famous American general who vowed "I shall return"

```
B  S  C  I  L  G  M
Y  T  E  J  N  Q  S
L  A  L  O  P  K  R
T  R  A  N  D  B  D
```

World War II began when Germany invaded this country.

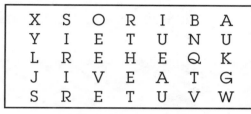

General MacArthur

World War II Country Codes

At the beginning of World War II, Americans lost many battles because the Japanese were able to intercept and understand their coded messages. Finally, a successful code was developed using an alphabet and terms from the Navajo language. The new code prevented the enemy from knowing of American plans and shortened the war in the Pacific. Here are some accepted country codes in common use today. Write the complete name for each one.

AU _____

CN _____

CA _____

GB _____

SU _____

BE _____

GR _____

FR _____

DE _____

IT _____

JP _____

BG _____

RO _____

HU _____

FI _____

EG _____

PL _____

NO _____

PH _____

NL _____

First Aid

Eight million copies of the *Red Cross First Aid Manual* were sold in 1942. Many students took first aid courses in school. The purpose was to make people more aware of safety hazards around them.

Here is a list of home hazards. Write how each one might affect a member of your family.

1. throw rugs_____

2. icy sidewalks _____

3. poor lighting_____

4. frayed electric cords _____

5. flammable materials near stoves_____

6. poisonous cleaning products _____

7. knives and scissors_____

8. guns _____

9. improperly stored medicines _____

10. articles piled on stairs _____

First Aid Kit

Today most families have a variety of medicines in their homes to take care of medical emergencies. Many people also carry a small first aid kit in their cars. Here is a list of readily available medications. Check your medicine cabinet or visit a drugstore. Write a brand name product for each of these categories.

- antiseptic _____

- bandages _____

- burn ointment _____

- cold remedy _____

- headache remedy _____

- eye drops _____

- cough medicine _____

- laxative _____

- analgesic cream _____

Three of a Kind

Below are various categories relating to the 1940s. List three or more people, places, or important dates associated with each category.

1. U.S. war heroes _____

_____

2. war rationed foods _____

_____

3. Nazi concentration camps _____

_____

4. women in the military _____

_____

5. women's fashions _____

_____

6. men's fashions _____

_____

7. jazz musicians _____

_____

8. Big Band vocalists _____

_____

9. artists _____

_____

10. writers _____

_____

11. world leaders _____

_____

12. athletes _____

_____

13. scientists _____

_____

14. cartoons/animation _____

_____

15. inventions _____

_____

66

The Cat in the Hat

In 1957 Dr. Seuss wrote *The Cat in the Hat*, a book with just 175 words, written in a rhyming style that appeals to both children and adults. In 1958 the popular cat returned for a sequel book titled *The Cat in the Hat Comes Back*.

Circle 10 words that rhyme with "cat" in this puzzle. The first two have been done for you.

```
C (A T) A (H A T) A P A T A F A T A
S A T A R A T A M A T B A T A B
A T A T H A T A F L A T C H A T
```

Dr. Seuss

Find the meaning for these items from *The Cat in the Hat* books.

1. theCAThat _____

2. the*fish*pot _____

3. the**wall**hall _____

4. the*Things*box _____

5. the*cake*tub _____

6. theRUGhall _____

Here are some others:

7. theMANmoon _____

8. the**shot**dark _____

9. the*cat*cradle _____

10. the*bird*bush _____

11. theLIGHTattic _____

12. the**bats**belfry _____

     #2601 20th Century Quiz Book

TV Families

The average American family in the 1950s had a mother, father, two children, and a dog. In 1954 RCA marketed the first color television. Use these clues to decide the favorite television shows of each family member.

The Smiths	Leave It to Beaver	I Love Lucy	Mickey Mouse Club	George Burns and Gracie Allen
Mother				
Father				
Judy, 12 years old				
Jimmy, 9 years old				

The Joneses	Lassie	What's My Line?	American Bandstand	Dragnet
Mother				
Father				
Billy, 15 years old				
Susie, 7 years old				

1. Mrs. Smith has red hair.

2. Mr. Smith always enjoys a good laugh.

3. Jimmy is always getting into mischief.

4. Judy watches this variety show each day after school.

1. Susie is allergic to cats but loves big dogs.

2. Billy loves to dance and listen to rock 'n' roll.

3. Mr. Jones is a policeman.

4. Mrs. Jones enjoys quiz shows.

Fads and Fashions—What Do They Mean?

Test your knowledge of the clothing and crazes of the '50s. Match each definition with a word or phrase from the word bank.

1. slim pants that reach to the calves

2. popular music style

3. another name for jeans

4. this medium brought news and sports events into America's homes

5. made from yards of nylon netting, this was worn under full skirts

6. series of hand movements done to music

7. frozen meal in an aluminum tray

8. outdoor movie theater

9. favorite meeting place for Beatniks

10. Alfred E. Newman's comical magazine

11. favorite two-toned footwear of teenage girls

12. term defining nonconformists of the decade

13. slim skirts

14. toy plastic disk thrown to a partner

15. long hair pulled back and held in place with a band

16. aerosol lubricant

17. slip-on shoes with space to hold a coin

18. slicked back male hairstyle

19. America's favorite fashion doll

20. short male military hairstyle

Word Bank

- duck tails
- crewcut
- Barbie
- penny loafers
- WD-40
- ponytail
- Frisbee
- pencils
- Beatniks
- saddle shoes
- Mad Magazine
- coffee house
- drive-in
- TV dinners
- hand jive
- petticoats
- television
- dungarees
- rock 'n' roll
- pedal pushers

Popular Music

Decode the pictures to reveal the names of songs or musicians of the fifties.

1 CH+ [duck] – D [strawberry] _____

2 [clock] [rock] _____

3 13 – THIR [angel] _____

4 4 x 4   [2000 lbs.] + S _____

5 [musical notes with chain] _____

6 F+ [hat] [hat] – H [domino] _____

7 [prisoner] [roll] _____

8 [crying woman] [crying pillow] _____

9 [broken heart] [HOTEL] _____

10 [birthday cake with candles] _____

Kids' Stuff

Kids' Stuff puzzles may include names of games, toys, entertainment, or food products from the period. The first number is from the vertical line on the left. The second is from the horizontal line across the top. Use the diagram to decipher the code.

	1	2	3	4	5
1	A	B	C	D	E
2	F	G	H	I	J
3	K	L	M	N	O
4	P	Q	R	S	T
5	U	V	W	X	YZ

Example: w = 53
d = 14

Example: 45-15-32-15-52-24-44-24-35-34

<u>television</u>

(1)   21-43-24-44-12-15-15 _____

(2)   33-11-14   33-11-22-11-55-24-34-15   _____   _____

(3)   12-11-43-12-24-15   14-35-32-32   _____   _____

(4)   43-35-13-31   '34'   43-35-32-32   _____   ____   _____

(5)   45-52   14-24-34-34-15-43   _____   _____

(6)   23-51-32-11 – 23-35-35-41   _____   –   _____

(7)   44-13-43-11-12-12-32-15 _____

(8)   13-23-11-43-32-35-45-45-15-'44   53-15-12   _____   _____

(9)   14-43.   44-15-51-44-44   _____.   _____

(10)   25-24-21   41-15-11-34-51-45   12-51-45-45-15-43   _____   _____   _____

Sports of All Sorts

Write the names of professional athletes in the spaces below to show their sport.

Baseball

1. _____

2. _____

3. _____

Football

1. _____

2. _____

3. _____

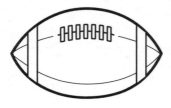

Basketball

1. _____

2. _____

3. _____

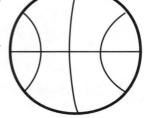

Soccer

1. _____

Name Bank

- Willie Mays
- Johnny Unitas
- Hank Aaron
- Jim Brown
- Mickey Mantle
- Otto Graham
- Wilt Chamberlain
- Pele
- Bill Russell
- Bob Cousy

Guinness Book of World Records

The McWhirter twins, Ross and Norris, were always fascinated with facts and records. They formed a company that did research for encyclopedias. They were also excellent athletes. Because of their background, the Guinness Brewery (Ireland) asked the McWhirters to co-author a record book that could be used to settle pub arguments. Their first book became a best seller in four months. In 1994 the book had worldwide sales of 74 million copies in 29 different languages. Use the 1998 volume to locate these record setters.

1. Who has won the most Oscars? _____

2. Who has hit the most home runs in a baseball season? _____

3. Who is the fastest man alive? _____

4. Who is the youngest female figure skating champion? _____

5. What is the best selling record album of all time?

_____

6. What is the longest running prime-time cartoon?

_____

7. What is the most frequently sung song in the English language? _____

8. What is the most widely syndicated comic strip?

_____

9. What is the world's best selling book?

_____

10. Who is the highest-ranking woman in the U.S. government? _____

11. Who was the oldest man to be elected president?

_____

12. Who is America's youngest billionaire?

_____

Here are the statistics for five record-setting fruits and vegetables. Match them.

- pumpkin _____
- potato _____
- strawberry _____
- watermelon _____
- green bean _____

1,061 pounds (477.5 kg); 48 3/4 inches (129.9 cm); 262 pounds (117.9 kg); 7 pounds, 6 ounces (3.3 kg); 8.17 ounces (228.8 g)

In the News

Use a reference book to help you find the items referred to in each of these stories.

1. _____ Charlotte Evangelist Returns to Hometown (1958)

2. _____ Quiz Show Caught in Scandal (1958)

3. _____ First Lady Steps Down Gracefully (1953)

4. _____ WWII Hero Named to Head Korean Forces (1950)

5. _____ Island Kingdom Becomes 50th State (1959)

6. _____ Couple Charged with Giving Secrets to Soviets (1951)

7. _____ Woman Arrested for Refusing to Give Up Bus Seat (1955)

8. _____ Amendment Limits Presidential Term (1951)

9. _____ Armistice Signed: Fighting Ends (1953)

10. _____ Arkansas' Central High School Is Integrated (1957)

11. _____ First African-American Woman Plays in the U.S. Open (1950)

12. _____ The "Yankee Clipper" Retires from Baseball with 361 Home Runs (1952)

13. _____ U.S. Launches Space Program with Satellite (1958)

14. _____ Anthropologist Discovers Human Fossils in Africa (1959)

15. _____ Plane Crash Kills Three Musicians (1959)

_____

_____

Word Bank

- Buddy Holly
- Ritchie Valens
- J. P. Richardson
- Hawaii
- *Explorer I*

- Mary Leakey
- Little Rock Nine
- Joe DiMaggio
- Korean War
- Bess Truman

- Althea Gibson
- 22nd Amendment
- Billy Graham
- *Twenty-One*
- Rosa Parks

- Ethel and Julius Rosenberg
- General Douglas MacArthur

Name Game

Read these clues about important people from the 1950s. Write a name in each blank to complete the chart.

	Location/Birthplace	**Event/Achievement**	**Name**
1.	38th parallel	led the Allied forces in Korean War	_____
2.	Montgomery, Alabama	arrested on bus ride	_____
3.	Topeka, Kansas	challenged school segregation	_____
4.	Tanzania, Africa	discovered Proconsul skull	_____
5.	Mount Everest	first to reach the top	_____
6.	Mount Vernon, New York	wrote *Charlotte's Web*	_____
7.	Sao Paulo, Brazil	soccer champion	_____
8.	Cuba	communist president	_____
9.	Suez Canal	Egyptian leader	_____
10.	Tupelo, Mississippi	king of Rock 'n' Roll	_____
11.	Richland Center, Wisconsin	innovative architect	_____
12.	Poland	doctor, polio vaccine	_____

Name Bank

- General Douglas MacArthur
- Pele
- Rosa Parks
- Fidel Castro
- Linda Brown
- Abdul Nassar
- Louis and Mary Leakey
- Edmund Hillary
- Norgay Tenzing
- Frank Lloyd Wright
- E.B. White
- Dr. Albert Sabin
- Elvis Presley

A Hero from the Fifties

During the mid-1950s, the United States witnessed the development of an extraordinary leader—a man who called out to the conscience of all America. He was a Christian minister whose congregation was not restricted to the rooms within a church. He called out to all peoples of this diverse, multi-ethnic nation—religious or nonreligious, inside churches or outside. Indeed, his call was to all humankind. Martin Luther King, Jr. rose to become a great symbol of justice and human equality, earning for himself an everlasting memory in the annals of this nation. Many politicians have been quick to take credit for passing civil rights laws, but Martin Luther King, Jr. was the inspirational leader who took this country by the hand to lead it to do the right thing—to "judge all humans not by the color of their skin but by the content of their character."

The following is a list of people and places associated with Martin Luther King, Jr.'s eventful life (which extended beyond the 1950s) in the service of the great cause of human equality. See if you can identify them with a few words describing how they were connected to the great hero.

1. Mohandas Gandhi _____

   _____

2. Coretta Scott _____

   _____

3. Rosa Parks_____

   _____

4. SCLC _____

   _____

5. Birmingham, Alabama _____

   _____

6. James Earl Ray _____

   _____

7. Andrew Young_____

   _____

8. Ralph David Abernathy _____

   _____

9. Selma, Alabama_____

   _____

10. Oslo, Norway (1964) _____

    _____

Alaska and Hawaii

Alaska and Hawaii became states in 1959. Read each clue. Write **A** if the statement is about Alaska, **H** if it is about Hawaii.

1. _____ Queen Liliuokalani

2. _____ Mauna Loa

3. _____ Juneau

4. _____ Eskimos

5. _____ William Seward

6. _____ Nene (state bird)

7. _____ Captain James Cook

8. _____ glaciers

9. _____ pineapples

10. _____ volcanoes

11. _____ January 3, 1959

12. _____ eight small islands

13. _____ willow ptarmigan (state bird)

14. _____ hibiscus (state flower)

15. _____ forget-me-not (state flower)

16. _____ August 21, 1959

17. _____ Mount McKinley

18. _____ North to the Future (state motto)

19. _____ Aleutian Islands

20. _____ Polynesian cultures

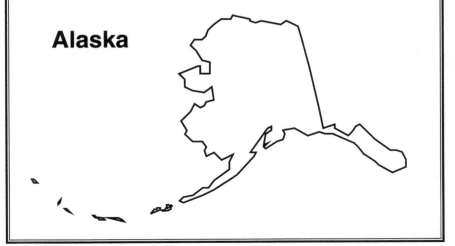

Alaska

Hawaii

#2601 20th Century Quiz Book

Happened in the Fifties

Use the diagram to decipher the code. The first number is from the vertical line on the left. The second is from the horizontal line across the top.

Example: w = 53   Example: 13-35-32-14   53-11-43
          d = 14   <u>cold</u>   <u>war</u>

	1	**2**	**3**	**4**	**5**
1	A	B	C	D	E
2	F	G	H	I	J
3	K	L	M	N	O
4	P	Q	R	S	T
5	U	V	W	X	YZ

1. **people**

   12-11-12-55

   _____

   12-15-11-45

   _____

2. **states**

   23-11-53-11-24-24
   11-32-11-44-31-11

3. **medicine**

   41-35-32-24-35

   _____

   31-24-14-34-15-55

   _____

4. **entertainment**

   13-35-32-35-43

   _____

   33-11-25-35-43

   _____

5. **religious leaders**

   12-24-32-32-55

   _____

   41-35-41-15

   _____

12-35-35-33-15-43-44

_____

22-15-34-15-43-11-45-24-35-34

_____

_____

_____

52-11-13-13-24-34-15

_____

45-43-11-34-44-41-32-11-34-45

_____

45-15-32-15-52-24-44-24-35-34

_____

32-15-11-22-51-15

_____

22-43-11-23-11-33

_____

25-35-23-34

_____

12-11-44-15-12-11-32-32

_____

54-54-24-24-24

_____

Sesame Street

Sesame Street premiered on PBS (the Public Broadcasting System) in 1969. It quickly became well known for teaching young children school-readiness skills. How much do you remember about *Sesame Street*? Read the clues and answer the questions below.

1. Cookie Monster's color __ __ __ __

2. Big Bird's color __ __ __ __ __ __

3. Ernie's friend __ __ __ __

4. Bert's friend __ __ __ __ __

5. Oscar loves this __ __ __ __ __

6. The Count loves these __ __ __ __ __ __ __ __

7. Elmo's color __ __ __

8. Kermit's color __ __ __ __ __

9. Rubber Duckie makes bath time lots of __ __ __

Can you help these children by following the path to show them how to get to Sesame Street?

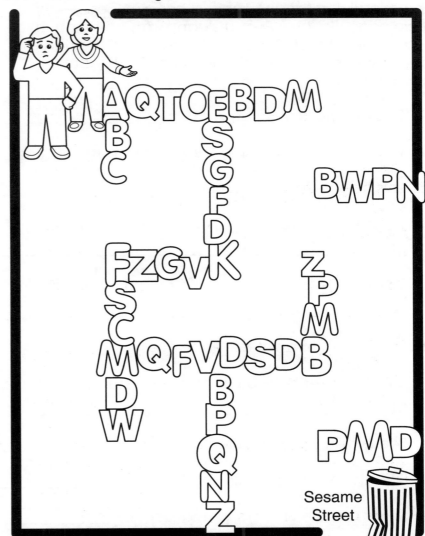

Sesame Street

All for Peanuts

Charles Schulz is the creator of the *Peanuts* comic strip. Some of his characters are named Charlie Brown; Linus; Schroeder; Lucy; and Snoopy, a beagle. Besides the comic page, Schulz's *Peanuts* gang can be found in children's books, clothing, and toys. Read the riddles and answer with the name of one of the *Peanuts* characters.

1. This beagle is a Flying Ace. _____

2. When she's around, the "Psychiatrist Is In." _____

3. This little yellow bird is Snoopy's friend. _____

4. This main character is always having some kind of problem. _____

5. This freckle-faced, brown-haired girl would like to be Charlie's girlfriend. _____

6. Dirt follows him wherever he goes. _____

7. Sally's "sweet babboo" is never without his favorite blanket. _____

8. Beethoven is his favorite composer. _____

9. She always calls Peppermint Patty "Sir." _____

10. She is Charlie Brown's younger sister. _____

Fill the name of a *Peanuts* character in each vertical line below.

Bonus: Name Charlie Brown's mystery love who is never seen in the comic strip.

_____

Picture Puzzle

Cut out the individual pieces to make a picture of an important event in American history.

Glue the completed puzzle onto a large piece of construction paper. Give the picture an appropriate title and find out the exact date the event took place.

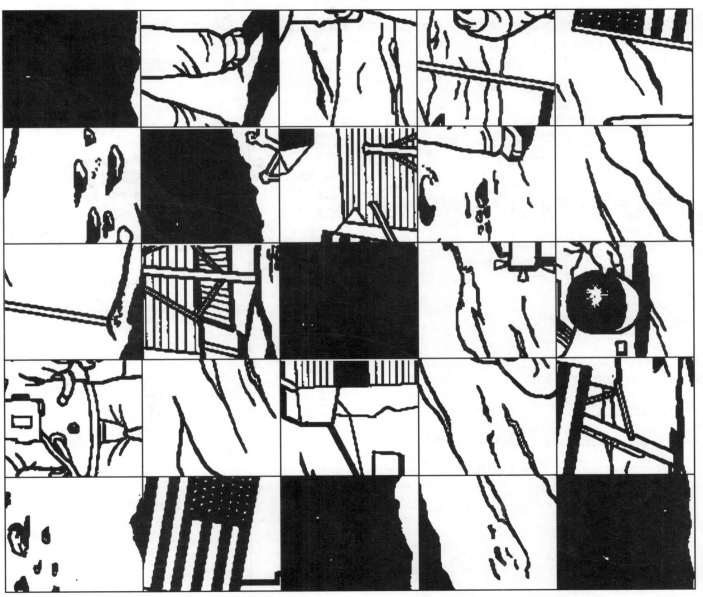

_____
title

_____
date

Beatlemania

The "Fab Four" appeared on *The Ed Sullivan Show* in 1964. These four boys from England had hordes of screaming fans. Write their first names in the puzzle below.

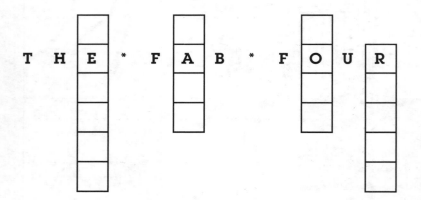

Match the first and last names.

1. _____ Harrison

2. _____ McCartney

3. _____ Lennon

4. _____ Starr

Decode these Beatles song titles.

1. Yellow

_____

2. Me Do

_____

3.  to Ride

_____

4. Lane

_____

5. Hard ☀ Z 🌙 ☆

_____

Popular Music

Decode the pictures to reveal the names of songs, groups, musicians, or events of the sixties.

Double Letters

Answer each clue with a word that contains double letters.

1. famous music festival _____

2. last name of Beatle John _____

3. 35th U.S. president _____

4. killed/murdered _____

5. home of Big Bird, Sesame _____

6. talk show host, Jack _____

7. miniskirt model _____

8. Cuban _____ Crisis

9. nanny in Oscar-winning film, Mary _____

10. freedom fighter _____

11. command module, moon flight _____

12. shot from a gun _____

13. Texas city _____

14. barrier which separated Berlin _____

15. plastic disk shaped toy _____

16. Austrian Olympic city _____

17. group that favored individual expression _____

18. racket sport _____

19. 1st African American on the U.S. Supreme Court (**double double**) _____

20. California center of the movie business (**double double**)

_____

The Torch Is Passed

John F. Kennedy, elected president of the United States in 1960, was shot while riding through the streets of a major city in Texas in 1963. Circle the correct answer to each of the following questions about Kennedy's assassination.

1 Time of Day	**2 Location**	**3 Date**
morning	Atlanta	October 15, 1963
afternoon	Cincinnati	November 22, 1963
evening	Dallas	September 7, 1963
midnight	San Diego	May 4, 1963
4 Weapon	**5 Scene**	**6 First Lady**
rifle	giving a speech	Ann
handgun	riding in motorcade	Rosemary
knife	eating dinner	Louise
poison	touring Europe	Jacqueline
7 Vice President	**8 Assassin**	**9 Burial Place**
Lyndon Johnson	Henry Ford	Forest Lawn
Barry Goldwater	John Wilkes Booth	Arlington
Richard Nixon	Lee Harvey Oswald	Memorial Park
Hubert Humphrey	Fidel Castro	Gate of Heaven
10 Nationality of Assassin	**11 Wounded Politician**	**12 Type of Car**
Cuban immigrant	John B. Connally	limousine
Soviet defector	Lyndon B. Johnson	sedan
American	Robert F. Kennedy	convertible
German	Dean Rusk	truck

Scrambled Names

The names of these people from the 1960s have been split into two-letter segments. The letters of the segments are in order, but the segments are scrambled. Put the pieces together to identify the personality. *Clues are given in parentheses.*

1. FK JO EN HN NE DY (president)

   _____

2. HU HU BE MP RT EY HR (senator)

   _____

3. PA AR LM NO ER LD (PGA golfer)

   _____

4. GA WE PO RY RS (U-2 pilot)

   _____

5. FL ON OY DP TE AT RS (boxer)

   _____

6. LY ON ND OH BJ ON NS (president)

   _____

7. RI AR CH DN ON IX (presidential candidate)

   _____

8. RR BA YG DW AT OL ER (senator)

   _____

9. WI AR LM UD PH OL (female track star)

   _____

10. E DI SN EY PR OIIT (movie star)

    _____

11. AL BS AN PA HE RD (astronaut)

    _____

12. BO YL BD AN (folk singer)

    _____

13. AN GR AM DM OS ES (artist of rural life)

    _____

14. LE AR ON DB ER TE NS IN (symphony conductor)

    _____

15. RT MA IN TH ER LU KI NG RJ (Civil Rights leader)

    _____

Name Game

Choose one word from each column to make the complete name of a famous person from the 1960s.

1. _____

2. _____

3. _____

4. _____

5. _____

6. _____

7. _____

8. _____

9. _____

10. _____

11. _____

12. _____

13 _____

14. _____

A	B	C
Richard	Milhous	Johnson
James	Edgar	King
J.	David	Moore
John	Harvey	Kennedy
Dwight	Luther	King
Billie	Scott	Oswald
Lee	Bird	Johnson
Lyndon	Jean	King
Martin	Tyler	Kennedy
Jacqueline	Bouvier	Eisenhower
Coretta	Baines	Ray
Mary	Jean	Hoover
Lady	Fitzgerald	Nixon
Norma	Earl	Baker

Bonus Questions

1. Name four U.S. presidents from the list.

   _____ _____ _____ _____

2. Name a married couple from the list who did not hold political office.

   _____

3. Name the actress in the list. _____

4. What was her professional name?_____

Civil Rights Movement

The 1960s were a time of action in the Civil Rights movement. Leaders were tired of waiting for legislation to improve their lives, so they planned sit-ins, boycotts, and marches to draw attention to their demands.

Circle the words or dates on the right that match the words on the left.

1.	**35th President**	Kennedy	Carter	Ford
2.	**"I Have a Dream . . ."**	M. L. King, Jr.	Newton	Evers
3.	**March on Washington**	1965	1963	1969
4.	**Watts Riots**	Cincinnati	Boston	Los Angeles
5.	**Dr. M. L. King, Jr.**	nonviolent	Muslim	violent
6.	**Civil Rights goal**	integration	segregation	occupation
7.	**Sit-in**	Washington Capitol rotunda	Woolworth's lunch counter	Atlanta bus station
8.	**Freedom Rides**	car sale	reduced plane fare	bus protest
9.	**Malcolm X**	Black Muslim	Catholic	Baptist
10.	**Stokely Carmichael**	black power	segregation	nonviolence
11.	**Huey Newton**	Freedom Rides	Black Panthers	NAACP
12.	**Rosa Parks**	March on Washington	Montgomery bus boycott	Freedom Rides
13.	**Medgar Evers**	NAACP	Supreme Court justice	famous civil rights lawyer
14.	**Ku Klux Klan**	nonviolent political group	supported desegregation	bombed black churches in the South
15.	**"Segregation now, segregation tomorrow, and segregation forever."**	George McGovern	Lyndon Johnson	George Wallace

88

Fly Me to the Moon

The United States joined the space race in the 1960s when President Kennedy promised to put a man on the moon. Write true or false in the blank before the statements. After each false statement, cross out the word or words that make it false and, on the line, write the word or words that make the statement true.

1. _____ The USSR sent Yuri Gagarin into space in 1969.

   _____

2. _____ The USSR's first spacecraft was called *Mir*.

   _____

3. _____ Early astronauts wore suits and ties into space.

   _____

4. _____ There is zero gravity in space.

   _____

5. _____ The surface of the moon is covered with forests.

   _____

6. _____ Alan Shepard flew in *Freedom 7*.

   _____

7. _____ Shepard's flight lasted two days.

   _____

8. _____ *Gemini 8* practiced docking techniques.

   _____

9. _____ *Gemini 4* astronauts did not leave their space capsule.

   _____

10. _____ Cape Canaveral is in Texas.

   _____

11. _____ Neil Armstrong, Buzz Aldrin, and Michael Collins made the first flight to the moon.

   _____

12. _____ The rocket used in the *Apollo 11* mission was called *Eros*.

   _____

13. _____ Buzz Aldrin was the first man to walk on the moon.

   _____

14. _____ It took three weeks to get to the moon.

   _____

15. _____ Americans watched the moonwalk on their televisions.

   _____

Categories

Read the clues and fill in the category.

1. Danang, Haiphong Harbor, Tet Offensive

2. Freedom Rides, sit-ins, Watts Riots

3. Martin Luther King, Jr.; John F. Kennedy; Medgar Evers

4. Neil Armstrong, Buzz Aldrin, Michael Collins

5. magnetron, fan, turntable

6. Linus, Snoopy, Lucy

7. *Help!, Revolver, A Hard Day's Night*

8. Fidel Castro, blockade, Kruschev

9. Michael Jordan, Brooke Shields, Whitney Houston

10. Sea of Tranquility, Sea of Rains, Sea of Cold

11. Harry Belafonte, Ossie Davis, Sidney Poitier

12. neon signs, Coca-Cola bottles, Campbell's soup cans

13. Medicare, Voting Rights Act, Civil Rights Act

14. communes, hippies, Woodstock

15. *Catch-22, To Kill a Mockingbird, Slaughterhouse Five*

Word Bank

- Vietnam War
- assassinated leaders
- parts of a microwave oven
- Beatles albums
- celebrities born in the 1960s
- African-American actors
- popular literary works
- moon landmarks
- subjects of Andy Warhol's paintings
- Cuban Missile Crisis
- *Peanuts* cartoon characters
- *Apollo 11* astronauts
- Civil Rights Movement
- Great Society
- Counterculture Movement

1900 1910 1920 1930 1940 1950 **1960** 1970 1980 1990

Analogies

To complete an analogy, you must first determine the relationship between the given items. The relationship may be person to birthplace, place to event, inventor to invention, etc. They are read as follows:

Fats Domino:"Blueberry Hill"::Chuck Berry:"Maybelline"

(Fats Domino is to "Blueberry Hill" as Chuck Berry is to "Maybelline.")

1. John Kennedy:Jackie::Lyndon Johnson:

   _____

2. Golda Meir:_____::John Kennedy:
   president

3. Marilyn Monroe:actress::Wilma Rudolph:

   _____

4. Cesar Chavez:California::Martin Luther King, Jr.:

   _____

5. Roberto Clemente:athlete::Neil Armstrong:

   _____

6. Charles Schultz:cartoons::Maurice Sendak:

   _____

7. Indira Ghandi:India::Golda Meir :

   _____

8. *Peanuts*:_____::100 cans of
   Campbell's soup: Andy Warhol

9. Neil Armstrong:USA::Valentina Tereshkova:

   _____

10. Sidney Poitier:_____::Roberto
    Clemente: Pittsburgh

11. *Where the Wild Things Are:* Maurice Sendak::
    *Silent Spring:*_____

12. Dr. Christian Barnard:_____::Louis
    Washansky: _____

13. Mao Tse-tung:China::Nikita Khrushchev:

    _____

14. _____:Soviet Union::Alan Shepard:
    USA

Canada's Centennial

Canada Day, July 1, 1967, marked the 100th anniversary of Canada. The country was born when four colonies—Quebec, Ontario, Nova Scotia, and New Brunswick—asked the British Parliament to pass the British North America Act (Constitution Act) creating a confederation of four provinces. Since then, six more provinces and two territories have joined the Dominion of Canada.

Read these world events from the 1960s. Underline five items that occurred in 1967.

1. The World's Fair was held in Montreal.

2. French President, Charles de Gaulle, pledged his support for a free Quebec.

3. Walt Disney died.

4. There was a war in Vietnam.

5. *Surveyor 3* landed on the moon and sent back photos.

6. Soviet tanks invaded Hungary.

7. Three astronauts were killed in a fire on *Apollo I*.

8. Neil Armstrong walked on the moon for the first time.

9. Civil rights demonstrators marched from Selma to Montgomery, Alabama.

10. The Kansas City Chiefs and the Green Bay Packers played in the first Super Bowl.

The letters "cent" refer to 100 (a *cent* is 1/100 of a dollar). Finish these words.

1. cent_____ period of 100 years

2. cent_____ one who is 100 years or older

3. cent_____ many-legged arthropod

4. cent_____ 1/100 of a meter

5. cent_____ temperature system with 100 units between boiling and freezing

6. cent_____ 100 year celebration

7. cent_____ to copy 100 times

8. cent_____ division into 100s

9. cent_____ a man commanding 100 men

10. _____cent one one-hundredth part

The Peace Corps

Fill in the blanks and fit the answers into the puzzle.

- The Peace Corps is a _____ organization.
- Volunteers _____ natives how to plant trees.
- A participant must be at least 18 years old and a U.S. _____ .
- Members agree to serve in the Corps for two _____ .
- They must respect the _____ of their host country.

- Peace Corps volunteers do not receive a large _____ .
- It is important that members enjoy _____ and helping people.
- Participants must leave their _____ and _____ behind.
- The Peace Corps is the "toughest job you'll ever _____ ."

African Independence

During the '50s and '60s, large European countries were encouraged to relinquish claim on their African colonies. Within a 30-year period, beginning in the fifties, 50 new states were created there. Here are some cities in Africa. Add the country name.

1. Ghirza, _____

2. Khartoum, _____

3. Casablanca, _____

4. Tozeur, _____

5. Accra, _____

6. Canakry, _____

7. Nairobi, _____

8. Abidjan, _____

9. Nouakchott, _____

10. Lilongwe, _____

11. Harare, _____

12. Banjul, _____

13. Libreville, _____

14. Mogadishu, _____

15. Giza, _____

16. Addis Ababa, _____

17. Dar es Salaam, _____

18. Djenne, _____

19. Dakar, _____

20. Lagos, _____

Countries

Libya, Senegal, Nigeria, Sudan, Morocco, Kenya, Cote d'Ivoire, Mauritania, Malawi, Zimbabwe, The Gambia, Gabon, Somalia, Egypt, Ethiopia, Tunisia, Ghana, Guinea, Tanzania, Mali

Headlines

Use a reference book to help you find the person(s) referred to in each of these stories. *There are more people listed in the word bank than you will need.*

1._____ Prime Minister Declares National Emergency—Quebec Separatists Terrorize Workers

2._____ American Swimmer Wins Seven Gold Medals at Munich Games

3._____ VP Resigns After Conspiracy Trial— Nixon Names Ford Successor

4._____ Acclaimed Artist Wraps Fence in San Francisco

5._____ Children's Author Contributes to *Free to Be You and Me* Project for *Ms.* Magazine.

6._____ Miniseries Explains Family History, Realistic Roots

7._____ *Annie Hall* Dominates Oscars—Director Stars with Diane Keaton

8._____ Russian Dancer Defects—Joins American Ballet Theater

9._____ Feminist Publisher Introduces New Magazine

10._____ First Black Woman Elected to U.S. Senate

11._____ First Lady Opens Clinic for Addicts

12._____ President Pardons Vietnam Draft Dodgers

13._____ President Resigns in Disgrace— Watergate Tapes Prove Conspiracy

14._____ Secretary of State Resigns After Failed Hostage Rescue

15._____ Three American Boxers Win Gold at Montreal Olympics

_____

_____

Word Bank

- Spiro Agnew
- Cyrus Vance
- Richard Nixon
- Pierre Trudeau
- Mark Spitz
- Michael Spinks
- Leon Spinks
- Sugar Ray Leonard
- Jimmy Carter
- Betty Ford
- Shirley Chisholm
- Christo
- Judy Blume
- Alex Haley
- Gloria Steinem
- Woody Allen
- Mikhail Baryshnikov
- Nelson Rockefeller
- Bob Woodward
- George McGovern
- Adam Clayton Powell, Jr.

Food Processors

The food processor was invented in 1971 by a Frenchman, Pierre Verdon. This versatile kitchen tool mixes, chops, and slices food quickly and safely. Decode the processed food names in the pictures below.

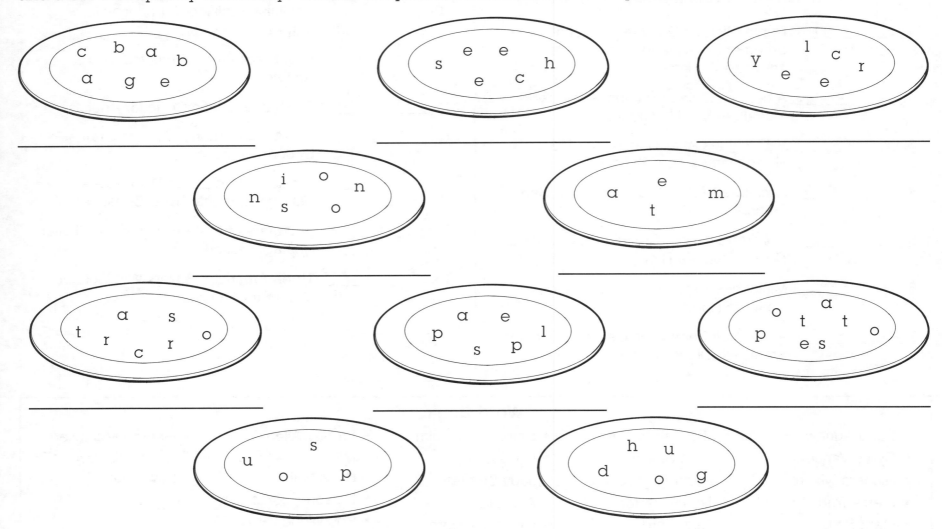

96

Calculator Fun

The affordable pocket calculator was introduced in 1970. Answer each of these problems with a calculator. When you have the answer, turn the calculator upside down to read an answer for each of the written clues. The first one is done for you.

1. (tool for outdoor watering) 7008 ÷ 2 = <u>3504 (hose)</u>

2. (tool for digging) 152 x 2 = _____

3. (petroleum) 142 x 5 = _____

4. (not the truth) 150+167 = _____

5. (dirt) 3265+3840 = _____

6. (boy's name) 15436 ÷ 2 = _____

7. (smaller than a mountain) 3857 x 2 = _____

8. (opposite of buy) 4361+3374 = _____

9. (not small) 206 x 3= _____

10. (tree limb) 1000 – 393 = _____

11. (necessary for running) 16911 ÷ 3 =_____

Sydney Opera House

Cross out the word that does not fit in each group.

1. Australian Ballet
   Sydney Symphony
   Australian Opera Company
   Metropolitan Guitar Series

2. concrete
   wood
   glass
   tile

9. singer
   dancer
   musician
   lawyer

10. president
    king
    queen
    prince

3. mast
   tires
   hull
   sails

4. movie
   concert
   ballet
   game

5. Canada
   Australia
   Great Britain
   India

6. Sydney
   Melbourne
   Quebec
   Cambria

7. harbor
   bay
   cove
   sand

8. architect
   builders
   doctor
   electricians

98

Amazon Rain Forest

In 1971 the Brazilian government began building a highway into the remote areas of the rain forest. They cut down trees and eroded the land. Much of the natural habitat was lost forever. Decode the names of these rain forest species by using letters that come after the ones you see (Z = A). Then classify the items as trees, plants, or animals.

1. JZONJ __ __ __ __ __

2. IZFTZQ __ __ __ __ __ __

3. SZOHQ __ __ __ __ __

4. OZKL __ __ __ __

5. UHMDR __ __ __ __ __

6. BZBSH __ __ __ __ __

7. QTAADQ __ __ __ __ __ __

8. AZMZMZ __ __ __ __ __ __

9. BZOXAZQZ __ __ __ __ __ __ __

10. RKNSG __ __ __ __ __

11. EDQM __ __ __ __

12. LZGNFZMX __ __ __ __ __ __ __ __

13. ZQLZCHKKN __ __ __ __ __ __ __ __ __

14. NQBGHC __ __ __ __ __ __

Trees

1. _____

2. _____

3. _____

4. _____

5. _____

Plants

1. _____

2. _____

3. _____

4. _____

Animals

1. _____

2. _____

3. _____

4. _____

5. _____

Earth Day

Cross out the words that complete these statements. The remaining word will complete the bonus sentence.

1. You can _____ water by taking short showers.

2. Use both sides of paper and then _____ it.

3. Plant a tree. They absorb _____ .

4. Trees give off _____ .

5. _____ products remain in landfills forever.

6. Write to factories about air and water
   _____ .

7. Support zoos that protect _____ .

8. Save _____ by lowering the thermostat.

9. Try not to buy or use products made from
   _____ .

10. Turn off _____ when you leave the room.

11. Don't use _____ on your lawn or garden.

12. Repair faucets that _____ .

13. Don't use _____ grocery bags.

14. Don't buy products that have many layers of
    _____ .

15. Do your part to keep _____ out of landfills.

Bonus:

The celebration of Earth Day was originated to protect the _____ .

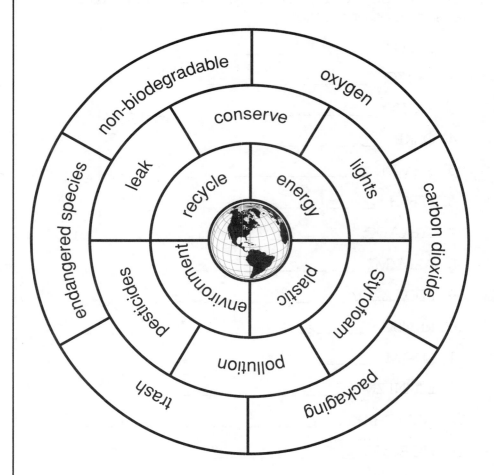

Words Within Words

Use the clues to help you fill in the blanks with a small word. The answers are words relating to important issues, events, or creations of the seventies. *Clues are given in parentheses.*

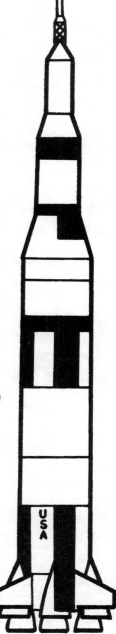

1. ___ ___ ___ T N A M (politics)

2. A ___ ___ ___ ___ M E N T (legislation)

3. E N ___ ___ ___ ___ ___ ___ E D (ecological issue)

4. C O N ___ ___ ___ ___ ___ ___ I O N (legislation)

5. I ___ ___ ___ H O S T ___ ___ ___ C R I S I S (politics)

6. ___ ___ ___ T H   D A Y (social issue)

7. E N V ___ ___ ___ ___ M E N T (social issue)

8. F E ___ ___ ___ ___ S M (politics)

9. E M ___ ___ ___ G O (politics)

10. C O M ___ ___ ___ E R (technology)

11. S P A C E ___ ___ ___ ___ ___ (technology)

12. F ___ ___ ___ I O N (cultural issue)

13. ___ ___ ___ ___ ___   D ___ ___ ___ ___ A C C O R D (politics)

14. W ___ ___ ___ R G ___ ___ ___ (politics)

15. A F ___ ___ ___ ___ A T I V E ___ ___ ___ I O N (social issue)

Space Exploration

Write true or false in the blank before the statements. After each false statement, write the word or words that make it true.

1. _____ *Apollo 13* landed safely on the moon.

   _____

2. _____ *Apollo 13's* lunar module provided backup
   power and oxygen. _____

3. _____ *Mariner 9* orbited Venus. _____

4. _____ *Apollo 16* and *17* were missions to the moon.

   _____

5. _____ *Skylab* crews observed the effects of zero
   gravity on small creatures.

   _____

6. _____ *Skylab* orbited the Earth for three years.

   _____

7. _____ *Skylab* had eight telescopes. _____

8. _____ *Mariner 10* was a weather satellite.

   _____

9. _____ *Viking 1* searched for life on Mars.

   _____

10. _____ *Voyager 1* discovered water on Mars.

   _____

Watergate Trivia

In 1972 seven men were accused of breaking into the National Democratic Headquarters. This scandal spread to include members of President Richard Nixon's cabinet and finally led to his resignation.

1. Who was the judge at the Watergate trial? _____

2. On what date were the Watergate burglars arrested?

   _____

3. How many men were indicted in the break-in? _____

4. How many minutes were erased from Nixon's phone tape? _____

5. Who erased the tape? _____

6. Name four members of the Nixon Administration who resigned because of allegations that the White House tried to cover-up the Watergate affair.

   _____

   _____

   _____

7. Name the *Washington Post* reporters who investigated the break-in.

   _____   _____

8. What was the code name of their source? _____

9. Who was the Chief Justice of the Supreme Court during the Watergate trial?

   _____

10. Why did the House Committee recommend Nixon's impeachment? _____

    _____

11. What did Nixon do when faced with impeachment?

    _____

12. Who became president after Nixon? _____

13. Who became the vice president? _____

14. Was Nixon punished? _____

15. How were the burglars punished? _____

Initials and Acronyms

These titles have been shortened to the first letters of each word. Use the clues to help you write the complete titles. *Clues are given in parentheses.*

1. C B (communication) _____

2. C R E E P (politics) _____

3. E R A (women's rights) _____

4. S A L T (politics) _____

5. I R A (politics) _____

6. C A T (medicine) _____

7. M R I (medicine) _____

8. P C (technology) _____

9. C D F (social issue) _____

10. E P A (legislation) _____

11. O P E C (oil crisis) _____

12. N O W (women's rights) _____

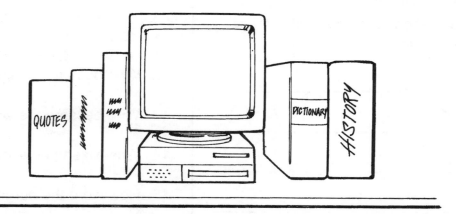

Think Metric

Congress called for a voluntary change to the metric system in 1975. Americans were used to the English system of measurement and resisted the change. They did not know how to compare a liter to a quart or how to measure distances in kilometers.

The metric system did not catch on in the United States, although it is used throughout the rest of the world.

The metric system uses a base ten. To convert from one level to another we use multiples of ten. Here are examples to show how easy it is to use the metric system.

These are the most common units of measurement:

- **gram** (weight)
- **meter** (length)
- **liter** (volume)

These prefixes are added to those terms:

k(ilo) = 1000 (For example, a kilogram = 1,000 grams.)

c(ent) = 0.01 (For example, a meter = 100 centimeters.)

m(illi) = 0.001 (For example, a liter = 1,000 milliliters.)

Use your knowledge of metrics to complete these problems.

1. 1 kg = 1000 g
   1 g = _____ g

2. 1,000mm = 1 m
   1 mm = _____ m

3. 1L = 1 kg
   1 mL = _____ g

4. 1 mL = 1 cm^3
   1 L = _____ cm^3

5. 1m^3 = _____ 1000 kg
   1 cm^3 = _____ g

Look at the Celsius (once called centigrade) thermometer. It is based on the metric system. 0° C is the freezing point of water and 100° C is the boiling point of water. Estimate the temperatures for the following:

6. normal room temperature _____

7. daytime in the Sahara Desert _____

8. summer at a Caribbean resort _____

9. spring day in Vancouver,
   British Columbia _____

10. inside your refrigerator _____

Quebec's Quiet Revolution

In 1974 and 1977, laws were passed in Quebec to make French the official language of the province. They felt their customs and traditions would be best preserved if the French language were used in business, commerce, and instruction. As a result, many people living in Quebec are bilingual, speaking both English and French.

Suppose you are an immigrant child in a French school. Translate these French words.

I. School Supplies

ciseaux _____

crayon _____

cahier _____

colle _____

crayons de couleur _____

II. Numbers 1-10 (Arrange them in order.)

une _____

quatre _____

trois _____

six _____

deux _____

cinq _____

huit _____

neuf _____

sept _____

dix _____

III. Colors

bleu _____

noir _____

brun _____

vert _____

orange _____

rouge _____

jaune _____

violet _____

IV. Common Expressions

Merci _____

Bonjour _____

Au revoir _____

Je regrette _____

Entrez _____

Dames _____

Hommes _____

Who Done It?

Solve these mysteries with names of famous people from the 1970s. Study the clues and then use a reference book to help find the answers.

1. Four student antiwar protesters were killed at Kent State University. Who done it? _____ (1970)

2. The United States President visited China. Who done it? _____ (1972)

3. President Richard Nixon is pardoned for his involvement in the Watergate scandal. Who done it? _____ (1974)

4. Bobby Riggs was defeated in a famous televised tennis match. Who done it? _____ (1973)

5. The President pardons Vietnam draft dodgers. Who done it? _____ (1977)

6. The Walkman, a portable radio and tape player, was marketed. Who done it? _____ (1979)

7. Fifty-two embassy workers were taken hostage. Who done it? _____ (1979)

8. The first woman competed in the Indy 5000. Who done it? _____ (1979)

9. An 18-year-old jockey won horse racing's Triple Crown. Who done it? _____ (1978)

10. A Hispanic player was MVP of the World Series. Who done it? _____ (1973)

11. The first affordable pocket calculator was developed.
Who done it? _____ (1973)

12. The Heimlich maneuver was developed to save choking victims.
Who done it? _____ (1974)

13. The first miniseries appeared on television. Who done it? _____ (1977)

14. The Panama Canal Treaty was signed, returning the canal to Panama by the year 2000. Who done it? _____ (1977)

15. An oil embargo caused high prices and gasoline rationing.
Who done it? _____ (1973)

R.I.P.

Here are sayings, or epitaphs, that might have appeared on the tombstones of famous people who died in the 1970s. Read the clues and fill in their names. Use a reference book to add the year each one was born.

1. As president, this man dropped the atomic bomb on Japan.

   Here lies _____ (_____–1972)

2. This man directed the Federal Bureau of Investigation.

   Here lies _____ (____–1972)

3. This woman won the Pulitzer Prize for her book *The Good Earth*.

   Here lies _____ (____–1973)

4. This man flew the *Spirit of St. Louis* nonstop from New York to Paris.

   Here lies _____ (_____–1974)

5. This man was called the King of Rock and Roll.

   Here lies _____ (_____–1977)

6. This man painted the covers for the *Saturday Evening Post* for 47 years.

   Here lies _____ (_____–1978)

7. This man led the Free French forces in World War II.

   Here lies _____ (____–1970)

8. This man, considered a saint by his people, was president of Argentina.

   Here lies _____ (____–1974)

9. This man was the deposed Emperor of Ethiopia.

   Here lies _____ (_____–1975)

10. This man was the communist leader of 800 million Chinese people.

    Here lies _____ (_____–1976)

Olympic People and Places

Cross out these people and places.

1. She set a world record in winning the 500-meter event in speed skating.

2. He is the first athlete to win 5 individual gold medals at one Olympics.

3. The site of the 1984 winter Olympics.

4. The site of the 1984 summer Olympics.

5. The site of the 1980 winter Olympics.

6. The site of the 1980 summer Olympics.

7. The site of the 1988 winter Olympics.

8. The site of the 1988 summer Olympics.

9. This track and field athlete participated in three Olympics.

10. She won silver and gold medals competing in the heptathlon.

11. This gymnast won the women's all-round gold medal in the 1984 Olympics.

12. She holds records in three freestyle swimming events.

13. He was the first diver to win springboard and platform events in two Olympics.

14. This wrestler won a gold medal in the freestyle super heavyweight division.

15. This male swimmer won 5 gold, 1 silver, and 1 bronze medal.

Bonus:

The remaining word names the country whose invasion by the Soviet Union caused President Jimmy Carter to ask the Olympic Committee to boycott the games in Moscow. This country was _____.

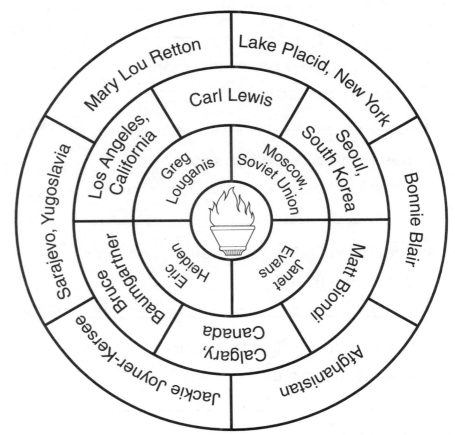

Mary Lou Retton — Lake Placid, New York — Carl Lewis — Seoul, South Korea — Bonnie Blair — Los Angeles, California — Greg Louganis — Moscow, Soviet Union — Matt Biondi — Afghanistan — Janet Evans — Calgary, Canada — Eric Heiden — Bruce Baumgartner — Jackie Joyner-Kersee — Sarajevo, Yugoslavia

Shel Silverstein

Shelby Silverstein worked as a cartoonist, poet, lyricist, composer, and playwright during his varied career. He had great skill rhyming words. Read the couplets and answer the questions with a title of one of Silverstein's children's books. The dates will help you.

1. Visit a library where reading is free,

   Check out a book called _____

   _____ _____ (1964)

2. It's fun to read a book with friends,

   Share a poem from _____ _____

   _____ _____ (1980)

3. This simple rule is always right:

   If you read in the attic, you'll need a light. _____

   _____ _____ _____ _____ (1980)

4. With Uncle Shelby there's always a laugh,

   You're sure to enjoy a_____

   _____ _____ _____ (1964)

5. Down or up, you'll have a ball

   When you learn the best way to fall.

   _____ _____ (1996)

Write the words that rhyme with Silverstein. The clues and the bank below to help you.

_____ ____ _____ (holiday colors)

_____ _____ (tired monarch)

_____ _____ (unhappy adolescent)

_____ ____ _____ (ratio heavy to light)

_____ _____ (pageant winner)

_____ _____ (aging cow)

_____ _____ (always kind)

_____ _____ (academic head)

_____ _____ (not always visible)

Rhyming Phrase Bank		
• seldom seen	• sleepy queen	• fat to lean
• red and green	• never mean	• old Holstein
• college dean	• angry teen	• beauty queen

Just a Phone Call Away

Use these "phone codes" (letters on the phone that correspond to numbers) to spell out words related to these clues.

1. Democtratic candidate for U.S. presidency in 1984 (666-3253) _____

2. Divided country after WWII (437-6269) _____

3. Citizens of the Soviet Union (768-4387) _____

4. Reusable aircraft (748-8853) _____

5. Rock concert to aid Ethiopia (548-3243) _____

6. Member of British royalty (242-7537) _____

7. Medicine (822-2463) _____

8. Female pop singer (623-6662) _____

9. Disaster at Chernobyl (682-5327) _____

10. East Berlin was this to the West (428-3929) _____

11. Nuclear arms race between the U.S. and Soviet Union (265-3927) _____

12. U.S. President (773-2426) _____

13. The people of China (244-6373) _____

14. Sale of arms to the Iran-Contras (722-6325) _____

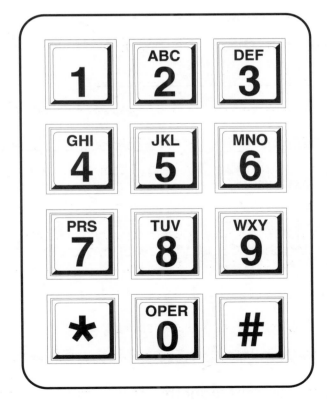

Challenger

The space shuttle *Challenger* exploded just over one minute into flight on January 28, 1986. Seven crew members, including one teacher, were killed.

1. The explosion was the biggest

   __ __ __ __ __ __ __ in the history of the U.S.
              1

   space program.

2. Millions of Americans watched the tragedy on the

   __ __ __ __ __ __ __ __ __ __.
           2

3. A faulty __ __ __ __ in a booster rocket caused
            3   4

   the explosion.

4. The teacher, Christa McAuliffe, was on her

   __ __ __ __ __ shuttle flight.
        5   6

5. More than two __ __ __ __ __ passed before
           7   8

   NASA launched another shuttle.

Word Bank

tragedy   seal   first   television   years

The Challenger explosion was a national

__ __ __ __ __ __ __ __
1   2   3   4   5   6   7   8

Challenge: What disasters happened at sea in 1912?

_____

1915?_____

Challenger Shuttle Disaster

The *Challenger* shuttle flew nine successful missions. On its tenth flight, on January 28, 1986, *Challenger* exploded less than two minutes after take-off, killing all the crew members. Write true or false in the blank before the statements. After each false statement, write the word or words that make it true.

_____ 1. Space shuttles have three parts: an orbiter, external tank, and solid fuel rocket boosters. _____

_____ 2. *Challenger* exploded on January 28, 1986. _____

_____ 3. *Challenger* had successfully completed six flights before the explosion. _____

_____ 4. Eight astronauts were lost aboard the space shuttle *Challenger*. _____

_____ 5. Christa McAuliffe was a high school social studies teacher on board the ill-fated flight. _____

_____ 6. George Bush was president at the time of the accident. _____

_____ 7. The explosion was caused by a gas leak from a faulty seal in the solid fuel rocket booster. _____

_____ 8. Cold weather at launch time contributed to the accident. _____

_____ 9. The disaster happened 74 seconds after liftoff. _____

_____ 10. A report said NASA had no idea about problems with the design of the shuttle. _____

_____ 11. The bodies of the astronauts were recovered and buried at Arlington National Cemetery. _____

_____ 12. The *Discovery* shuttle was launched successfully 2 ½ years following the *Challenger* disaster. _____

Lady Liberty

The centennial celebration for the Statue of Liberty was held on July 4, 1986. The two-year project included replacing 1,600 wrought iron bands that hold the copper skin to the frame, replacing the torch, and installing an elevator. The four-day celebration which followed included fireworks, concerts, festivals, and the swearing in of 5,000 new citizens.

Complete the problems below to uncover information about the size of the statue.

1. **weight** $5,000 \times 90 =$ _____ pounds

2. **height** (heel to top of head) $58 + 83 =$ _____ feet

3. **index finger** (length) $5,272 \div 659 =$ _____ feet

4. **inside steps** $7,392 \div 44 =$ _____ steps

5. **distance across the eye** $1.3 + 1.2 =$ _____ feet

6. **nose** (length) $18 - 13.5 =$ _____ feet

7. **right arm** (length) $(6 \times 9) - 12 =$ _____ feet

8. **mouth** $(12 \times 9) - 105 =$ _____ feet

9. **waist** $(4 \times 7) + 7 =$ _____ feet

These words are part of the poem "The New Colossus" that is written on the tablet that the statue holds. Change the words in parentheses so that the poem reads correctly.

"Give me your (sleepy), your (rich), your huddled masses yearning to breathe (enslaved). The (pitiful) refuse of your teeming (water). Send these, the (resident), tempest-tost to me. I lift my (table) beside the (silver) (window)!"

Create a Word

Choose a part of a word from each column to form a new word related to the eighties. Each part may be used only once. The first part of each word is in column A. Write the new words in the blanks.

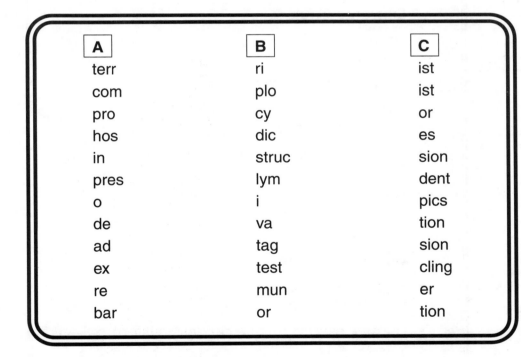

A	**B**	**C**
terr	ri	ist
com	plo	ist
pro	cy	or
hos	dic	es
in	struc	sion
pres	lym	dent
o	i	pics
de	va	tion
ad	tag	sion
ex	test	cling
re	mun	er
bar	or	tion

1. _____

2. _____

3. _____

4. _____

5. _____

6. _____

7. _____

8. _____

9. _____

10. _____

11. _____

12. _____

Presidential Puzzle

Fill in the blanks and fit the answers into the puzzle spaces.

- He was the 40th _____ of the United States.
- He appointed the first _____ to the Supreme Court.
- He wanted to cut _____ for all Americans.
- John Hinckley attempted to _____ him.
- His wife is named _____ .
- He sent aid to freedom fighters in _____ .
- Like many other presidents, he thought it was important to balance the federal _____ .
- He was a movie _____ .
- He signed a treaty with the _____ to reduce nuclear arsenals.
- He proposed a missile defense system called _____ _____.

Fabulous Females

Many women made history by being the first to achieve a particular status in their fields during the 1980s. Use the clues to name these fabulous, famous females.

1. first female in the U.S. Supreme Court

2. first woman chosen to be a vice-presidential candidate by a major U.S. political party

3. first female prime minister of Great Britain

4. first lady of the United States 1981-1989

5. first lady of the United States 1989-1993

6. first woman chief of Cherokee nation

7. first female prime minister of India

8. woman president of the Philippine Islands

9. first American woman to fly into space

10. first female television news co-anchor

Lists

The events, items, and people listed here were newsmakers in the 1980s. Read the lists and fill in the titles.

1. _____

    Greg Louganis   Matt Biondi

    Janet Evans   Eric Heiden

    Bonnie Blair

2. _____

    Dr. Sally Ride   John W. Young

    Robert L. Crippen   Dr. Judith Resnick

    Michael J. Smith

3. _____

    John Lennon   Michael Jackson

    Whitney Houston   Madonna

    Led Zepplin

4. _____

    Mikhail Gorbachev   Deng Xiaoping

    Ronald Reagan   Margaret Thatcher

    Anwar el-Sadat

5. _____

    Sandra Day O'Connor   Geraldine Ferraro

    Nancy Reagan   Barbara Bush

    Wilma Mankiller

6. _____

    Exxon *Valdez*   Chernobyl

    Challenger   Mount Saint Helens

    famine in Ethiopia

7. _____

    Soviet troops   guerillas

    Kabul   Jimmy Carter

    peace accord

8. _____

    Ronald Reagan   Mikhail Gorbachev

    START I   warheads

    missiles

9. _____

    Oliver North   Ronald Reagan

    Nicaragua   Sandinistas

    Contras

10. _____

    East/West Germany   barbed wire

    border   freedom

    outdoor art galleries

Analogies

To complete an analogy, you must first determine the relationship between the given items. The relationship may be person to birthplace, place to event, inventor to invention, etc. They are read as follows:

Ronald Reagan:Illinois::George Bush:Massachusetts

(Ronald Reagan is to Illinois as George Bush is to Massachusetts.)

1. *Indian in the Cupboard*:_____::*Light in the Attic*:Shel Silverstein

2. TWA Flight 847:Rome::Pan Am Flight 103:_____

3. Mikhail Gorbachev:_____::Anwar el-Sadat:Egypt

4. Meryl Streep:_____::Barbara Walters:television

5. Chernobyl:steam explosion::_____:volcanic eruption

6. Eric Heiden:_____::Mary Lou Retton:gymnast

7. *Enterprise*:first orbiter::_____:first shuttle

8. answering machine:_____::VCRs:TV shows

9. John Lennon:Beatles::Michael Jackson:_____

10. Prince Charles:England::Lech Walesa:_____

11. Labor:Conservative::Democratic:_____

12. Jimmy Carter:_____::Ronald Reagan:George Bush

Techno-Terms

Use this code to identify these techno-term definitions.

A	C	D	E	F	I	L	M	N	O	R	S	T	W
1	2	3	4	5	6	7	8	9	10	11	12	13	14

1. __ __ __ __ __ __ __ __
   12 10 5 13 14 1 11 4
   computer programs

2. __ __ __ __ __ __ __ __
   6 9 13 4 11 9 4 13
   network of computers linked by cable phone lines

3. __ – __ __ __ __
   4   8 1 6 7
   electronic mail

4. __ __ – __ __ __
   2 3   11 10 8
   compact disk – read only memory

5. __ __ __ __ __ __ __
   8 10 9 6 13 10 11
   computer screen

6. __ __ __ __ __
   8 10 3 4 8
   telephone connection to the Internet

7. Cross out all the letters (except L) that appear twice in the puzzle below to reveal the name of the founder of Microsoft, a large computer firm.

B	C	I	R	L
L	R	G	D	A
T	D	E	C	S

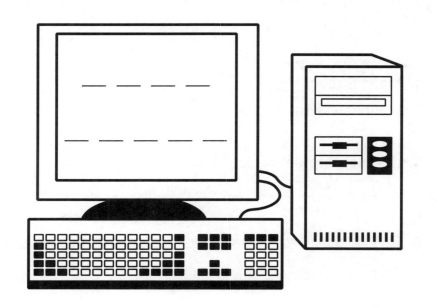

Celebrity Plates

A car license plate can tell something about its owner. Decode these plates to reveal clues to the names of television and movie stars from the 1990s.

1. **GR8HERO** _____

2. **MSCLEAN** _____

3. **NO1TALK** _____

4. **THE*COS** _____

5. **TOOLMAN** _____

6. **CITYGUY** _____

7. **MRFGUMP** _____

8. **7-4*DAY** _____

9. **THEROCK** _____

10. **GR8LAFF** _____

11. **BIGJOKE** _____

12. **MSPERKY** _____

13. **FAV*LADY** _____

14. **BIGSTAR** _____

Hillary Clinton Writes

First Lady Hillary Clinton has worked for improvement in the education and living conditions of America's children. In 1996 she published a book explaining her ideas. Starting with the letter "I," write every third letter printed around the picture on the lines below. The result will be the title of her award winning book.

(I)   I   L   T   S   L   T

I
I   A   E
A   D   A
D   V   A
V   R   A
R   L   G
L   A   K
A   O   I   S   T   H   E   E   C

Book Title

" I _____

_____

_____

_____

_____ "

McCaughey Septuplets

On November 19, 1997, Bobbi McCaughey gave birth to healthy septuplets at the Iowa Methodist Medical Center. Mr. and Mrs. McCaughey, who live in Carlisle, Iowa, welcomed their seven new babies to the world with enthusiasm. The family received help from church and family members as well as a new house and lots of free baby products from manufacturers around the United States.

Use these numbers to decode the babies' names.

1	7	14	21	28	35	42	49	56	63	70	77	84	91	98	105
K	**E**	**N**	**T**	**H**	**A**	**L**	**I**	**S**	**Y**	**B**	**R**	**D**	**O**	**J**	**X**

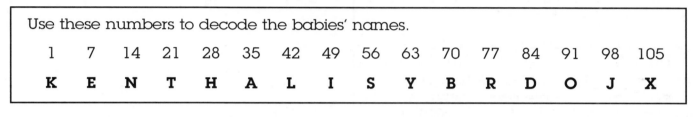

```
___  ___  ___  ___  ___  ___  ___      ___  ___  ___  ___  ___  ___      ___  ___  ___  ___  ___  ___
 1    7   14   14    7   21   28       35   42    7  105   49   56        1    7   42   56    7   63
```

```
            ___  ___  ___  ___  ___  ___  ___      ___  ___  ___  ___  ___  ___  ___
             14   35   21   35   42   49    7       70   77   35   14   84   91   14
```

```
            ___  ___  ___  ___  ___  ___      ___  ___  ___  ___
             14   35   21   28   35   14       98   91    7   42
```

The prefix *sept* means seven. What is the meaning of these words that begin with *sept*?

Draw a line to match each word with a correct definition.

1. septennial   ▪ a group of seven people
2. septet   ▪ a word with seven syllables
3. September   ▪ to multiply by seven
4. septisyllable   ▪ the seventh month of the early Roman calendar
5. septuagenarian   ▪ to copy seven times
6. septuple   ▪ a person between 70 and 80 years of age
7. septuplicate   ▪ occurring every seven years

Michael Jordan

It is said that Michael Jordan is the best basketball player who has ever lived, but as a sophmore, he did not even make his high school team. Michael's hard work and determination have allowed him to excel at his sport.

Answer these questions and score 2 or 3 points as indicated. If you answer every question correctly, you will know the number of triple-doubles Michael has scored in his career. A triple-double occurs when a player scores at least 10 points, 10 rebounds, and 10 assists in a game.

1. How tall is Michael Jordan? (3 points)
2. Name Michael's wife. (3 points)
3. Name Michael's mother. (3 points)
4. Name Michael's older son. (3 points)
5. Name Michael's daughter. (3 points)
6. In what state was Michael born? (3 points)
7. What university did he attend? (2 points)
8. In what years did he play on U.S. Olympic basketball teams? (2 points)
9. What other professional sport did he try? (2 points)
10. What is Michael's middle name? (2 points)
11. What was Michael's NBA team? (2 points)
12. Total career triple-doubles _____

Calculate Michael's basketball statistics.

1. $(4 \times 7) - 5 =$ _____ (Michael's jersey number)
2. $14 + 33 + 28 - 12 =$ _____ (Career-high points scored in a playoff game)
3. $78 - 30 - 20 =$ _____ (Career triple-doubles)
4. $(2 \times 5) - 4 =$ _____ (Chicago Bulls championship teams)
5. $(7 \times 5) - 30 =$ _____ (NBA Most Valuable Player)
6. $(3 \times 3) + 2 =$ _____ (NBA All-Star games)
7. $(2 \times 6) - 2 =$ _____ (Seasons leading the league in scoring)
8. $9,759 \times 3 =$ _____ (Total points scored in career)
9. $18,246 \div 6 =$ _____ (Most points scored in a single season)
10. $(6 \times 9) + 15 =$ _____ (Most points scored in a regularseason game)
11. $(8 \times 8) - 19 =$ _____ (Jersey number Michael used after his return from baseball)
12. $104 \div 8 =$ _____ (Michael's shoe size)

The Right Stuff

Lt. Col. John Glenn (United States Marine Corps, Retired) was born in Cambridge, Ohio. When he was 40 years old, he became the first American to orbit the Earth. Glenn returned to space almost 37 years later when, on October 29, 1998, he became the oldest person ever to fly into space. His mission was to do experiments on the effects of aging.

Use reference materials to find these facts about John Glenn.

Every answer will be a number.

1. The month (number) of John Glenn's space shuttle *Discovery* flight was _____ .

2. The number of days *Discovery* orbited the Earth was _____ .

3. The year of Glenn's return to space, 199_____.

4. Glenn piloted the *Friendship* _____ as a *Mercury 6* astronaut.

5. The year of the *Friendship* flight was 19_____ 2.

6. The *Friendship* flight lasted almost _____hours.

7. The number of terms John Glenn was an Ohio State senator was _____ .

8. The number of times *Friendship* orbited the Earth was _____ .

9. Senator and Mrs. Glenn have _____ children.

10. The year of John Glenn's birth was 192_____ .

John Glenn

"Godspeed, John Glenn."

Who spoke those famous words?_____

Current Events

Analyze these clues to determine the events.

1. France and England worked together on this project.
   - It is more than 30 miles (50 km) from end to end.
   - Machines with steel teeth were used to cut through soft rock.
   - It connects Folkestone, England, and Calais, France.
   - This underwater transportation was opened May 6, 1994.

   What is the event? _____

2. The Berlin Wall has fallen; the Soviet influence is gone.
   - People cheered and families are reunited.
   - Chancellor Helmut Kohl is the head of the new government.
   - Berlin will be the new capital.
   - East and West are one nation again.

   What is the event? _____

3. Iraqi tanks cross the border.
   - U.N. leaders condemn the invasion.
   - The U.S. sends war ships.
   - The palace is burned; the emir escapes to Saudi Arabia.

   What is the event? _____

4. Human barricades save the Russian Parliament.
   - Three Muscovites are killed by tanks.
   - The Communist Party is shut down.
   - Party leaders resign.
   - Boris Yeltsin is a hero.

   What is the event? _____

5. His democratic reform movement began the new system.
   - Eleven former Soviet republics became the Commonwealth of Independent States.
   - Control of the Soviet nuclear arsenal passed to Yeltsin.
   - The red flag was lowered over the Kremlin; his job was abolished.

   What is the event? _____

6. Terrorists attack New York City.
   - The Twin Towers garage is believed to be the site of the bomb.
   - Five are killed; many suffer smoke inhalation.
   - Fire rages in commuter train station.

   What is the event? _____

Lists

The events, items, and people listed here were all important in the 1990s. Read the lists and fill in the titles.

1. _____

   U.S. terrorism   Murrah Federal Building
   truck bomb   Timothy McVeigh
   Terry Nichols

2. _____

   Kuwait   Saudi Arabia
   Norman Schwarzkopf   Iraq
   Saddam Hussein

3. _____

   Louis Farrakhan   black men
   responsibility   Rev. Benjamin Chavis
   Washington, D.C.

4. _____

   Shannon Lucid, NASA   *Mir* Space Station
   Russian cooperation   scientific experiments
   cosmonauts

5. _____

   rhyming verse   strong beat
   no melody   MTV
   sampling

6. _____

   Muslims   Serbs
   Croats   bombs
   peace negotiations

7. _____

   coup   Yeltsin
   Gorbachev   Kremlin
   perestroika (economic reform)

8. _____

   Gaza Strip   West Bank
   PLO, Yasir Arafat   Yitzhak Rabin
   Shimon Peres

9. _____

   Nelson Mandela   segregation
   African National Congress   white minority rule
   independence

10. _____

   U.S. Dept. of Defense   e-mail
   on-line   download
   modem

Desert Storm

In the Gulf War, called Operation Desert Storm, Iraqi troops invaded the small neighboring country of Kuwait in order to control their oil resources. International troops assembled in nearby Saudi Arabia and engaged in air and land battles for several months. Middle Eastern countries were torn in their loyalties to Saddam Hussein, the Iraqi leader, and the powerful Western governments. As in any war, many people were injured, lives were lost, and much property was damaged.

Label the map of the Middle East with these Gulf War locations:

Red Sea, Israel, Jordan, Iraq, Kuwait, Bahrain, Qatar, United Arab Emirates, Persian Gulf, Saudi Arabia.

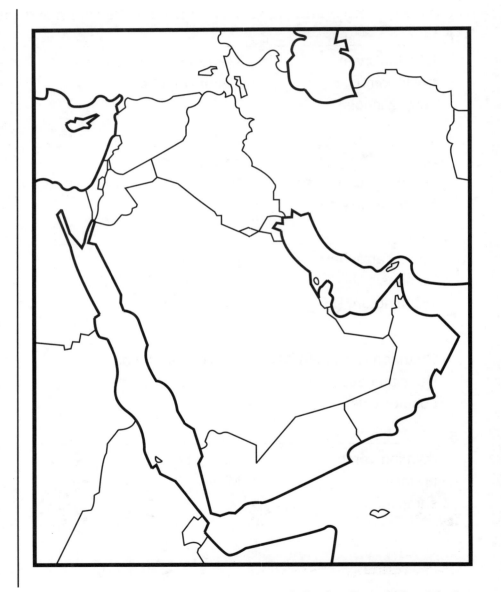

1. _____

2. _____

3. _____

4. _____

5. _____

6. _____

7. _____

8. _____

9. _____

10. _____

128

Gulf War

Code	25	26	1	2	3	4	5	6	7	8	9	10	11	12	13	14	15	16	17	18	19	20	21	22	23	24
Key	A	B	C	D	E	F	G	H	I	J	K	L	M	N	O	P	Q	R	S	T	U	V	W	X	Y	Z

Analyze the code to find the answers.

Example: 7-16-25-15 = <u>Iraq</u>

1. **Code name**

   13-14-3-16-25-18-7-13-12   2-3-17-3-16-18

   _____   _____

   17-18-13-16-11

   _____

2. **People**

   17-25-2-2-25-11   6-19-17-17-3-7-12

   _____   _____

   12-13-16-11-25-12   17-1-6-21-25-16-24-9-13-14-4

   _____   _____

   14-16-3-17-7-2-3-12-18   5-3-13-16-5-3   26-19-17-6

   _____   _____   _____

3. **Places**

   26-25-5-6-2-25-2   9-19-21-25-7-18

   _____   _____

   21-25-17-6-7-12-5-18-13-12   2-1

   _____, ____

4. **Weapons**

   17-1-19-2   11-7-17-17-7-10-3

   _____   _____

   17-18-3-25-10-18-6   4-7-5-6-18-3-16

   _____   _____

   18-13-11-25-6-25-21-9   1-16-19-7-17-3

   _____   _____

   11-7-17-17-7-10-3

   _____

   1-13-11-26-25-18   25-7-16-1-16-25-4-18

   _____   _____

Analogies

To complete an analogy, you must first determine the relationship between the given items. The relationship may be person to birthplace, place to event, inventor to invention, etc. They are read as follows:

Michael Jordan:basketball::Tiger Woods:golf

(Michael Jordan is to basketball as Tiger Woods is to golf.)

1. Janet Reno:Harvard Law School::Hillary Clinton:

_____

2. Ross Perot:_____::Bill Clinton: Democrat

3. Louis Farrakhan:Nation of Islam::Rev. Benjamin Chavis:_____

4. _____:Magic Johnson::hockey:Wayne Gretzky

5. Bill Gates:_____::Ted Turner:CNN

6. Johnny Carson:Iowa::Oprah Winfrey:

_____

7. Janet Reno:attorney general::Madeline Albright:

_____

8. Boris Yeltsin:Russia::_____:United States

9. Michael Johnson:running::Dan Jansen:

_____

10. Pete Sampras:_____::Oprah Winfrey:microphone

11. George Bush:_____::Bill Clinton: Al Gore

12. Yitzhak Rabin:_____::Nelson Mandela:South Africa

13. *Titanic*:_____::*Schindler's List*:Steven Spielberg

14. Tony Blair:_____::Benjamin Netanyahu:Israel

Web Sites

These imaginary Web sites could lead you to information about famous people of the 1990s. Answer each one with a name.

1. www.russia.pres.gov _____

2. www.firstlady.US _____

3. www.mmmarch.wash/LF _____

4. www.masters1997/PGA _____

5. www.chmn/USJCS/Bush _____

6. www.1stfem/attorneygen.US _____

7. www.reformpty.pres. _____

8. www.bullsstar/MJ.nike _____

9. www.windows/MS _____

10. www.woman/NASA.*Mir* _____

11. www.daytime/talk/abc _____

12. www.primeminister.Isr/Nobel _____

13. www.pres.safrica _____

14. www.ussr/fmr.pres _____

15 www.leader/PLO _____

Initials and Acronyms

These titles have been shortened to the first letters of each word. Use the clues to help you write the complete titles. *Clues are given in parentheses.*

1. U S S R _____
   (world—Eurasia)

2. P L O _____
   (world—Mideast)

3. U N _____
   (world)

4. A N C _____
   (civil rights—Africa)

5. C D-R O M _____
   (technology)

6. D I N K S _____
   (social)

7. W W W _____
   (technology)

8. N A T O _____
   (world politics)

9. M S - D O S _____
   (technology)

10. N A S A _____
    (science)

11. I B M _____
    (technology)

12. P G A _____
    (sports)

13. N A A C P _____
    (civil rights)

14. R O T C _____
    (army)

15. E D S _____
    (technology)

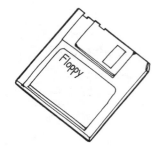

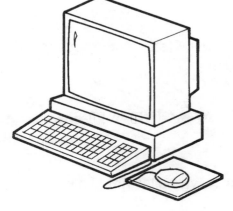

Top Ten Best-Selling Children's Books

Read these top ten lists compiled by Publishers Weekly. Identify the book titles.

Top Ten Best-selling Hardcover Books for Children

10. This 1960 book by Dr. Seuss is about a school of colorful seafood.

9. Charles Tazewell wrote this book in 1946 about a tiny heavenly being.

8. This popular book from 1957 is about a chapeau-wearing feline.

7. A "doctor" wrote this book in 1960 about unusually colored breakfast foods.

6. Babies and toddlers enjoy the soft feel of Dorothy Kunhardt's interactive book from 1940.

5. This story of a little red boat that traveled the world was first published in 1955.

4. This 1947 book by Kathyrn and Byron Jackson tells the story of a loose-skinned pachyderm.

3. A little train engine learns what it means to become a big locomotive in this 1945 classic.

2. The first of Beatrix Potter's classic stories is about a mischievous bunny in a blue jacket.

1. The number one best selling hardcover children's book of all time is Janette Sebring Lowrey's story of a slow moving puppy written in 1942.

Top Ten Best-selling Paperback Books for Children

10. Laura Ingalls Wilder wrote this story about a pioneer family living in the forest.

9. Ms. Wilder wrote a second best seller about pioneers living on the flat grassland.

8. This 1971 book, by Scott O'Dell, is based on a true story, "The Lost Woman of San Nicolas."

7. An unearthly visitor changed the lives of Meg and Charles in this sci-fi best seller by Madelaine L'Engle.

6. A boy's love for his prize-winning coonhounds is the basis for this story by Wilson Rawls.

5. The joys and fears of a preadolescent girl are the topic for Judy Blume's 1972 book.

4. A boy learns about courage and self respect in this 1983 book by Jack Schaefer.

3. This book by Judy Blume give readers a humorous look at life in the fourth grade.

2. In this 1968 book, S.E. Hinton gives us a look inside (and outside) gangs.

1. The number one best selling paperback children's book of all time is E.B. White's story of the unlikely friendship between a pig and a spider.

Popular Pairs

See if you can name the missing partner in each of these entertainment duos.

1. Laurel and _____

2. Tom and _____

3. Popeye and _____

4. Mickey and _____

5. Beauty and the _____

6. Mutt and _____

7. Lady and the _____

8. Sonny and _____

9. Wallace and _____

10. Sylvester and _____

11. Lone Ranger and _____

12. Barbie and _____

13. Homer and _____

14. Laverne and _____

15. Mork and _____

16. Batman and _____

17. Superman and _____

18. Starsky and _____

19. Lucy and _____

20. Ozzie and _____

Famous Pairs

Find out who these famous pairs are by using the clues given below.

1. These archaeologists uncovered fossils of early man at Olduvai Gorge, Tanzania.

   They are _____

2. These German immigrants collaborated on the *Curious George* books.

   They are _____

3. These Argentine leaders are remembered as saints in their native country.

   They are _____

4. Charged with treason for passing secrets to the Soviet Union during World War II, this couple was sentenced to death.

   They are _____

5. These comedians had a show business career in vaudeville, radio, and television.

   They are _____

6. This first couple lived in the White House longer than any other.

   They are _____

7. These brothers wrote the music and lyrics for many popular songs of the 1920s.

   They are _____

8. These explorers were the first to reach the North Pole.

   They are _____

9. This former president and first lady once had careers as movie actors.

   They are _____

10. This royal couple's divorce caused concern about the future of Britain's monarchy.

    They are _____

11. These women of Northern Ireland won the Nobel Peace Prize for their work against violence.

    They are _____

12. These men worked in Panama to make it possible for America to build the Panama Canal.

    They are _____

O Canada

Find 10 mistakes in this map of Canada.

Famous Canadians

Write the names of these Canadians in the proper spaces to show their accomplishments.

Wayne Gretzky, Anna Pelletier, William Shatner, Matthew Perry, Donovan Bailey, Michael J. Fox, Roberta Bondar, Pierre Trudeau, Alanis Morisette, Brian Mulroney, Shania Twain, Celine Dion, Terry Fox, Jean Chretien

Prime Ministers

1. _____

2. _____

3. _____

TV and Movie Stars

1. _____

2. _____

3. _____

Athletes

1. _____

2. _____

3. _____

First Female Astronaut

1. _____

Popular Music Stars

1. _____

2. _____

3. _____

Marathon of Hope

1. _____

This Land Is Your Land

Find 16 mistakes in this map of the United States.

138

Man-made World Landmarks

Read the information and name the landmark.

1. Year—1994   Country—Japan
   Problem: There is limited space in this small country.
   Solution: Engineers built this synthetic island.
   Landmark: _____

2. Year—1959   Country—Australia
   Problem: City needed a fine arts center.
   Solution: Architects designed a structure compatible with the natural surroundings.
   Landmark: _____

3. Year—1970   Country—Egypt
   Problem: The Nile River flooded valuable farmland.
   Solution: A dam and reservoir provide electricity and irrigation.
   Landmark: _____

4. Year—1994   Country—England/France
   Problem: There was no bridge across the English Channel.
   Solution: An underwater tunnel was built for cars and trains.
   Landmark: _____

5. Year—1975   Country—Canada
   Problem: Toronto was renovating its downtown area.
   Solution: Workers built one of the world's tallest freestanding structures.
   Landmark: _____

6. Year—1937   Country—United States
   Problem: There was no bridge across San Francisco Bay.
   Solution: The water is spanned by a six-lane bridge with sidewalks.
   Landmark: _____

7. Year—1931   Country—United States
   Problem: The Colorado River caused flooding and crop loss.
   Solution: A large project including a dam, reservoir, and power plant.
   Landmark: _____

8. Year—1914   Country—Panama
   Problem: There was no efficient water route between the Atlantic and Pacific Oceans.
   Solution: A water passage was built through Central America.
   Landmark: _____

9. Year—1988   Country—Japan
   Problem: The country needed a way for trains to travel between Honshu and Hokkaido.
   Solution: The world's longest transportation tunnel was built.
   Landmark: _____

10. Year—1941   Country—United States
    Problem: An artist was asked to create a tourist attraction in the Black Hills.
    Solution: The heads of four U.S. Presidents were carved into the mountainside.
    Landmark: _____

Australian Animals

Some of the most unusual animals in the world are native to Australia. Use these clues to identify some of them.

1. Duckbilled, egg-laying, fur-covered animal with webbed feet. P __ __ __ __ __ __ S

2. Egg laying mammal, with long claws, long snout, and quills. E __ __ __ __ __ A

3. Wild dog with a bushy tail, preys on livestock. D __ __ __ O

4. Marsupial that eats grass, bushes, and roots. W __ __ __ __ T

5. Macropod, this type of kangaroo lives in the open. W __ __ __ __ __ Y

6. Nocturnal marsupial, eats only eucalyptus leaves. K __ __ __ A

7. Small, rat-like creature, eats insects and worms. B __ __ __ __ __ __ __ T

8. Heavy, wingless bird. E __ U

9. Bird with a loud, laughing voice. K __ __ __ __ __ __ __ __ __ A

10. Large, featherless, flightless bird. C __ __ __ __ __ __ __ Y

11. Nocturnal marsupial that eats every part of its prey. T __ __ __ __ __ __ __ __ N D __ __ __ L

12. Large animal with one hump, eats tree leaves and fruit. C __ __ __ L

Word Bank

platypus, echidna, wallaby, koala, bandicoot, dingo, wombat, emu, kookaburra, Tasmanian Devil, camel, cassowary

---

Picture the Presidents

Decode the pictures to reveal the names of U.S. presidents. Write their last names.

1. George

_____

2. Jimmy  + ter

_____

3. Rutherford B. 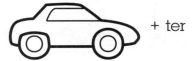 + es

_____

4. Ulysses S. Gr +

_____

5. Franklin   P +  + ce

_____

6. Zachary  + or

_____

7. James K.   P +  − y

_____

8. John  + ler

_____

#2601 20th Century Quiz Book

Quotes and Slogans

Match the president to his quote or campaign slogan. There are more presidents listed than there are campaign slogans.

1._____ *I like Ike.*

2._____ *Four more lucky years*

3._____ *LBJ for the USA*

4._____ *Speak softly and carry a big stick.*

5._____ *Four more years of a full dinner pail*

6._____ *I'm voting for Betty's husband.*

7._____ *The buck stops here.*

8._____ *The morning in America.*

9._____ *Read my lips: No new taxes!*

10._____ *We must build a bridge to the future.*

Teddy Roosevelt

Harry Truman

Ronald Reagan

- Gerald Ford
- Woodrow Wilson
- Richard Nixon
- Franklin D. Roosevelt
- Bill Clinton
- Teddy Roosevelt
- George Bush

- Harry Truman
- William McKinley
- Ronald Reagan
- Lyndon B. Johnson
- Dwight Eisenhower
- Herbert Hoover
- Calvin Coolidge

Nicknames

Match the real names of the people in the word bank with their nicknames. *(Clues are given in parentheses.)*

1. The Sultan of Swat _____ (baseball)

2. The Black Pearl _____ (soccer)

3. Ike _____ (president)

4. Dutch _____ (president)

5. The Cos _____ (entertainer)

6. The Iron Lady _____ (prime minister)

7. The King of Late Night _____ (entertainer)

8. The Golden Bear _____ (golf)

9. The Wizard of Menlo Park _____ (inventor)

10. Bubba _____ (president)

11. Satchmo _____ (musician)

12. The Georgia Peach _____ (baseball)

13. The Little Tramp _____ (entertainer)

14. America's Sweetheart _____ (entertainer)

15. Scarface _____ (gangster)

Word Bank

- Babe Ruth
- Pelé
- Dwight Eisenhower
- Ronald Reagan
- Bill Cosby
- Mary Pickford
- Charlie Chaplain
- Ty Cobb
- Louis Armstrong
- Bill Clinton
- Margaret Thatcher
- Johnny Carson
- Jack Nicklaus
- Thomas Edison
- Al Capone

Web Sites

These imaginary Web sites could lead you to information about famous people, places, or events in the twentieth century. Find the person, place, or thing that would be closely linked to the following imaginary Web sites.

1. www.daviscup.com _____

2. www.worldcup.1958 _____

3. www.volcanoes.us.washington _____

4. www.oilspill.alaska.exx/val _____

5. www.reunification.ger/wall _____

6. www.tuskegee.sch.edu_____

7. www.saturday-evening-post.covers.art_____

8. www.cherokee.nation.fem.chief _____

9. www.landmarks.syd.au_____

10. www.nasa.moonwalk.gov_____

11. www.vatican-city/head _____

12. www.1stfem/SCourt.US _____

13. www.greatsociety/US.pres _____

14. www.scandal/resign.Nixon _____

15. www.lennon-mccartney/music.group _____

144

Equations

In an equation, one side always equals the other. Fill in these equations to find out what in twentieth century history is equal to each other. (*Clues are given in parentheses.*)

1. 9 = P on a BT (*1900 World Series*) = players on a baseball team

2. 9 = S integrating LRCHS (*civil rights*) =

3. 4 = P on MR (*national memorial in South Dakota*) =

4. 4 = S killed at KSU (*1970 Vietnam War protest*) =

5. 110,000 = JA confined during WWII (*1940s war*) =

6. 50 = S in the U.S. (*North America*) =

7. 18 = LA to V in the U.S. (*politics*) =

8. 58,000 = A died in VW (*1960s–70s war*) =

9. 4 = B recorded R&R music (*1960s entertainment*) =

10. 159 = C in the UN (*world politics*) =

11. 3 = times JG orbited E (*space technology*) =

12. 43 = JFK's age when elected P (*1960s politics*) =

13. 4 = times FDR elected P (*1940s politics*) =

14. 28 = years G was divided by the BW (*cold war*) =

15. 3 = AP in WWII (*1940s war*) =

Fashion Show

Write the decade for each style of clothing.

1._____

2._____

3._____

146

Fashion Show (cont.)

Write the decade for each style of clothing.

4._____

5._____

6._____

R.I.P.

Here are sayings, or epitaphs, that might have appeared on the tombstones of famous people throughout the twentieth century. Read the clues and fill in their names.

1. With Bible and hatchet she fought the sale of liquor and tobacco.

   Here lies _____ 1846 –_____

2. Her pictures and stories about small woodland animals bring enjoyment to young children.

   Here lies _____ 1866 –_____

3. As a professional baseball player, this "Georgia Peach" won 12 batting titles.

   Here lies _____ 1886 –_____

4. America's sweetheart appeared in 194 films and won an Academy Award in 1928.

   Here lies _____ 1893 –_____

5. This military scout and sharpshooter starred in his own Wild West show.

   Here lies _____ 1846 –_____

6. This "Little Tramp" made American audiences laugh in silent movies.

   Here lies _____ 1889 –_____

7. She was the first women to fly solo across the Atlantic Ocean.

   Here lies _____ 1897 –_____

8. He was the first African American to integrate major league baseball and play in a World Series.

   Here lies _____ 1919 –_____

9. This "Argentine Joan of Arc" married the president even though she had not finished high school.

   Here lies _____ 1919 –_____

10. Half of a husband-wife comedy team, her career began on the vaudeville stage.

    Here lies _____ 1906 –_____

Word Bank

- Gracie Allen—1964
- Evita Peron—1952
- Jackie Robinson—1972
- Charlie Chaplin—1977
- Buffalo Bill Cody—1917
- Mary Pickford—1979
- Amelia Earhart—1937
- Beatrix Potter—1943
- Carry Nation—1911
- Ty Cobb—1961

Answer Key

1900s

Page 4—Mother's Day
1. woman
2. spring
3. England
4. carnation
5. Wilson
6. Anna Jarvis

Page 5—Memory Game
Answers will vary.

Page 6—Who's Driving
1. Kipling, Potter, etc.
2. Peary, Henson
3. Carry Nation
4. Andrew Carnegie
5. Picasso, Cassatt, etc.
6. McKinley, T. Roosevelt
7. Ida McKinley, Edith Roosevelt
8. Wilbur and Orville Wright
9. Queen Victoria
10. Lenin, etc.
11. Evans and Knossos
12. Ford

Page 7—Analogies
1. automobile
2. temperance
3. New York
4. soccer
5. tank
6. Russia
7. Einstein
8. *The Tale of Peter Rabbit*
9. Cubism
10. radio
11. Father's Day
12. Native Americans
13. United States
14. China
15. theater productions

Page 8—Presidential Diplomacy
Speak softly and carry a big stick.
1. 5
2. Panama
3. Rough Riders
4. youngest
5. Nobel Peace Prize

Page 9—Scrambled Names
1. Elizabeth Stanton
2. Teddy Roosevelt
3. Mohandas Gandhi
4. Albert Einstein
5. Sigmund Freud
6. Rudyard Kipling
7. Pablo Picasso
8. Will Rogers
9. Anna Jarvis
10. Andrew Carnegie
11. Wilbur Wright
12. Lucy Maud Montgomery

Page 10—Scout Law
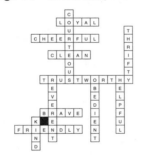

Page 11—Australia
1. prisoners
2. Aborigines
3. Canberra
4. states
5. continent
6. Britain
7. Gold
8. Sydney

Page 12—Australian Independence

Page 13—Three of a Kind
Answers will vary.

Page 14—Nobel Prize Winners
1. Lech Walesa
2. Desmond Tutu
3. Woodrow Wilson
4. Lester Bowles Pearson
5. Albert Einstein
6. Theodore Roosevelt
7. Linus Pauling
8. Mother Teresa
9. Marie Curie
10. Ivan Pavlov
11. Martin Luther King, Jr.
12. Jane Addams
13. Rudyard Kipling
14. Max Planck
15. Albert Schweitzer
16. Winston Churchill
17. Gabriela Mistral

Page 15—Headlines
1. Lyman Frank Baum
2. Andrew Carnegie
3. Oklahoma Territory
4. William McKinley

5. Panama
6. Theodore Roosevelt
7. New York City
8. Henry Ford
9. Boston
10. William Howard Taft
11. Robert Peary
12. Geronimo
13. London
14. Rudyard Kipling
15. Ellis Island
16. Arizona

Page 16—R.I.P.
1. Henri de Toulouse-Lautrec 1901
2. Paul Gaugin 1903
3. James Whistler 1903
4. Frederick Bartholdi 1904
5. Jules Verne 1905
6. Henrik Ibsen 1906
7. Paul Cezanne 1906
8. Nicolai Rimsky-Korsakov 1908
9. Joel Chandler Harris 1908
10. Antonin Dvorak 1904

1910s

Page 17—Take Your Vitamins
A healthy diet has many different kinds of food. You should eat fruits and vegetables, cereal and bread, dairy products, and lean meat every day. Be careful not to overeat foods high in sugar and fat. Eating the right foods will help you grow strong and healthy.

Answer Key *(cont.)*

Page 18—Zipper King
1. bookbag
2. suitcase
3. duffel
4. tent
5. shorts
6. sleeping bag
7. upholstery
8. purse
9. jeans
10. dress
11. boots
12. overalls
13. raincoat
14. jacket

Page 19—Father's Day
1. Sunday
2. papa
3. kids
4. Nixon
5. June
6. Spokane
7. Sonora Louise Smart Dodd

Page 20—Kindergarten
1. red
2. green
3. nine
4. ten
5. end
6. dirt
7. rain
8. train
9. trade
10. tea
11. ink
12. dark
13. grain
14. dinner
15. tangerine

Page 21—Picture Puzzle

Answer: Uncle Sam

Page 22—Who Done It?
1. Vincenzo Perugia
2. Roald Amundsen
3. Madame Marie Curie
4. Dr. William Gorgas
5. Gavrilo Princip
6. Jack Johnson
7. German submarine
8. Bolshevik forces
9. French officials
10. Max Planck
11. Benito Mussolini
12. Germany and Allied leaders
13. Woodrow Wilson
14. Constantine
15. Turks of the Ottoman Empire

Page 23—Labor Reform
1. limiting child labor
2. shortened work day
3. safer working conditions
4. increased wages
5. creation of labor unions
6. worker strikes
7. industrial revolution
8. mass production
9. job security
10. pension funds

Page 24—Slang Terms and Nicknames
Slang
1. big shot
2. cutting remark
3. it's a cinch
4. joyride
5. lousy
6. lowbrow
7. peachy
8. spill the beans
9. string along
10. sweat shop
11. doughboys
Nicknames
12. Lloyd George, Orlando, Wilson, Clemenceau
13. Jack Dempsey
14. Charlie Chaplin
15. Mary Pickford
16. Ty Cobb
17. William F. Cody
18. Manfred von Richtofen
19. Florence Nightingale
20. Theodore Roosevelt

Page 25—Panama Canal
1. Central America
2. malaria, yellow fever
3. France
4. Theodore Roosevelt
5. lock and lake
6. George Goethals

7. Woodrow Wilson
8. William Gorgas
9. Alcon
10. toll
11. international
12. channel
13. isthmus
14. causeway
15. Panama Canal Treaty

Page 26—News of the Decade
1. 1915
2. 1917
3. 1913
4. 1912
5. 1918
6. 1911
7. 1914
8. 1917
9. 1912
10. 1912
11. 1910
12. 1911
13. 1911
14. 1917
15. 1919

Page 27—Disaster on the High Seas
1. *Titanic*
2. *Carpathia*
3. *California*
4. New York City
5. Iceberg
6. Captain Edward Smith
7. Belfast, Ireland
8. John Jacob Astor

Answer Key (cont.)

Page 28—Telegrams
1. kinetophone
2. Panama Canal
3. *Lusitania*
4. Vladimir Lenin
5. *Titanic*
6. Olympics
7. Father's Day
8. epidemic (pandemic)
9. alcohol
10. right to vote
11. League of Nations
12. child labor

Pager 29—The Great War
1. Allies
2. tanks
3. enemy
4. submarine
5. army
6. force
7. march
8. target
9. invade
10. attack
11. Germany
12. Balkans

Page 30—A Tale of Two Presidents
1. Wilson
2. Taft
3. Wilson
4. Taft
5. Taft
6. Taft
7. Taft
8. Wilson
9. Wilson
10. Taft
11. Wilson
12. Wilson
13. Wilson
14. Taft
15. Taft

1920s

Page 31—Cartoon Genius
1. Mickey Mouse
2. Snow White
3. Cinderella
4. Pinnochio
5. Minnie Mouse
6. Donald Duck
7. Pluto
8. Goofy
9. Dumbo
10. Sleeping Beauty

Page 32—Food Chain
1. cereal
2. lettuce
3. eggs
4. soup
5. peanut
6. tomato
7. onion
8. noodles
9. spinach
10. hamburger
11. raisins
12. sausage

Page 33—I've Got Your Number
1. 19
2. 18
3. 30
4. 60
5. 25
6. 4
7. 3
8. 5
9. 42
10. 5¢
11. 17
12. 54
13. 7
14. 8¢
15. 6

Page 34—Egyptian Excavations
1. Valley of the Kings
2. Luxor, Egypt
3. Howard Carter
4. Lord Carnarvon
5. embroidered robes
6. gilt statues
7. precious stones
8. Pharaoh's tomb
9. four chariots
10. hieroglyphic writing
11. golden mummy case

Page 35—Product Slogans
1. zipper
2. Wrigley's chewing gum
3. Band-Aids
4. Kleenex
5. Scotch Tape
6. potato chips
7. frozen vegetables
8. permanent wave
9. Eskimo Pie
10. Welch's grape jelly

Page 36—Words Within Words Within Words
(The following are possible answers. Students may find others.)
1. went, ties, roar, ring
2. are, car, care, scar
3. tea, pot, do, me, an, can, and, scan
4. rag, rage, get
5. road, as, cast, broad
6. dine, in, net
7. tank, tan, an, am, ham, men
8. ant, tar, arc, an
9. in, dust, try, us
10. reside, side, dent, den

Page 37—Aussie Speak
1. The *lazy person* lost his job as town *garbage collector*.
2. His *wife* had no *money* to buy food for the family.
3. Three *children skipped kindergarten* because they were sick.
4. The family was driving out of town when their *car engine* ran out of gasoline.
5. *Kangaroos* bounce around the *wilderness*.
6. The *woman* had an *excellent* idea for killing a *snake*.
7. *Children* like eating *candy* and *crackers* with their *friends*.
8. The old *man* went to the *drugstore* to buy medicine.
9. The poor *man* left his *umbrella* and *flashlight* on the train.
10. Our *family* uses an *elevator* to reach our third floor apartment.

Page 38—Create-a-Word Social Issues
immigration, suffragism, temperance, alcohol, bootlegging, demonstrate, prejudice, creationism, religion, amendment, bigotry, liberty

Answer Key *(cont.)*

Page 39—Three Clues
1. Babe Ruth
2. "Shoeless" Joe Jackson
3. Warren G. Harding
4. Sacco and Vanzetti
5. Tutankhamen
6. Vladimir Lenin
7. John Scopes
8. Harry Houdini
9. Charles Lindbergh
10. Duke Ellington
11. Amelia Earhart
12. Emperor Hirohito
13. Coco Chanel
14. Commander Richard Byrd
15. Alexander Fleming

Page 40—The Twenties
1. Al Capone
2. Prohibition
3. flappers
4. Jazz
5. Ku Klux Klan
6. Oct. 29, 1929
7. speakeasies
8. Jack Dempsey, Lou Gehrig
9. Model T
10. Gloria Swanson, Greta Garbo
11. Amelia Earhart, Gertrude Stein
12. zipper, pop-up toaster
13. Harding, Coolidge
14. Margaret Sanger, Ethel Byrne
15. Clarence Darrow, William Jennings Bryan
Nickname: *Roaring Twenties*

Page 41—Sound and Silence
1. I, sound
2. C, silent
3. F, silent
4. A, silent
5. H, silent
6. J, silent
7. K, silent
8. G, silent
9. L, sound
10. E, silent
11. D, silent

12. B, sound

Page 42—Headlines
1. Hoover
2. Babe Ruth
3. Albert Einstein
4. Bessie Coleman
5. Sonja Henie
6. Arthur A. Schomburg
7. John Scopes
8. Charlie Chaplin
9. Charles Lindbergh
10. Henry Ford
11. Gutzon Borglum
12. Gabriela Mistral
13. Howard Carter
14. Richard Byrd
15. Pablo Picasso

1930s

Page 43—Follow the Yellow Brick Road
1. L. Frank Baum
2. Metro-Goldwyn-Mayer
3. Judy Garland
4. Toto
5. Kansas
6. Tornado
7. Heart
8. Brain
9. Courage
10. "Over the Rainbow"
Bonus: *Gone With the Wind*

Page 44—Double Letters
1. depression
2. apple
3. million
4. Roosevelt
5. Russia
6. Chancellor
7. Nessie
8. Jesse
9. Grimm
10. Sherwood
11. jazz
12. Banner

13. Hoover
14. Missouri
15. Hull
16. Anna
17. Benny Goodman
18. Glenn Miller

Page 45—A Great Educator
"Enter to learn, depart to serve."

Page 46—The Star-Spangled Banner
see, dawn's, hailed, twilight's, stripes, stars, perilous, ramparts, streaming, rocket's, bombs, proof, flag, star, land, home
1. 1776
2. 1777
3. 1795
4. 1848
5. 1864
6. 1912

Page 47—Athletes
1. Sonja Henie—Figure Skating
2. Helen Wills Moody—Tennis
3. Jesse Owens—Track and Field
4. Joe Louis—Boxing
5. Lou Gehrig—Baseball
6. Mildred "Babe" Didrikson Zaharias—Golf, Track and Field

Page 48—Supermarket Shopping
1. potatoes and gravy
2. fish and chips
3. cake and ice cream
4. soup and crackers
5. peas and carrots
6. meat and potatoes
7. peanut butter and jelly
8. beans and franks
9. lettuce and tomatoes
10. chips and dip
11. ham and eggs
12. bread and butter
13. baked beans
14. cold cuts
15. French fries
16. pepperoni pizza
17. pumpkin pie

18. cheddar cheese
19. strip steak
20. crispy crackers
21. candy cane
22. frosted flakes
23. rump roast
24. green grapes
25. canned corn
26. spaghetti sauce
27. black beans

Page 49—Olympic Competitions
Berlin Olympics
Los Angeles medals

Page 50—Words Within Words
1. Great Depression
2. labor unions
3. prohibition
4. migration
5. helicopter
6. Hoovervilles
7. unemployment
8. president
9. Social Security
10. Adolf Hitler

Answer Key *(cont.)*

Page 51—Quotes in Codes
1. "A chicken in every pot, a car in every garage."
2. "The only thing we have to fear is fear itself."
3. "Our greatest primary task is to put people to work."

Page 52—Creations of the Thirties
1. Monopoly
2. yo-yo
3. roller skates
4. jump rope
5. frozen food
6. Spam
7. Wonder Bread
8. *Snow White and the Seven Dwarfs*
9. television
10. Superman

Page 53—Trivia
1. Herbert and Lou Hoover
2. Franklin and Eleanor Roosevelt
3. Lou Henry Hoover
4. George Washington Carver
5. Jane Addams
6. Shirley Temple
7. Woody Guthrie
8. Babe Didrikson
9. Sergei Prokofiev
10. John Steinbeck
11. Edward VIII
12. Superman

Page 54—Analogies
1. Harvard
2. highways
3. gangster
4. investors
5. Margaret Mitchell
6. track and field
7. clarinet
8. song
9. quintuplets
10. Germany
11. actress
12. Alexander Calder
13. Metropolitan Opera
14. Franklin Roosevelt

15. Wallis Simpson

1940s

Page 55—Picture Memory
Answers will vary

Page 56—Curious George
1. banana
2. yellow
3. the zoo
4. seagulls
5. sailors
6. firemen
7. prison
8. through an open door
9. balloons
10. blue
11. three mice eating cheese
12. white cat
13. two
14. dictionary
15. blue slippers

Page 57—Harry S Truman
The buck stops here.
1. Japan
2. 1945
3. Hiroshima and Nagasaki
4. *Enola Gay*
5. Potsdam Treaty

Page 58—Made in the U.S.A.

Page 59—That's Entertainment
big band music
theater

Page 60—Read All About It
1. 12/7/41	6. 5/10/40
2. 1/20/45	7. 6/6/44
3. 10/29/40	8. 1/27/45
4. 2/19/45	9. 4/30/45
5. 4/12/45	10. 8/14/45

Page 61—Men and Women of World War II

Men
John—sailor, Pearl Harbor
Edward—general, Normandy
Thomas—lieutenant, Germany
James—sergeant, southern Italy

Women
Rosie—airplane factory
Clara—Red Cross
Harriet—home
Betty—USO
Sarah—bank

Page 62—World War II Lists
1. Allied Forces
2. Axis Powers
3. atomic bomb
4. home front
5. rationed items
6. heroes
7. world leaders
8. aircraft
9. battles
10. Holocaust

Page 63—World War II
1. Pearl Harbor
2. rationing coupons
3. Rosie the Riveter
4. Winston Churchill
5. Franklin Roosevelt
6. Axis Powers
7. Douglas MacArthur
8. Poland

Page 64—World War II Country Codes
AU – Australia
CN – China
CA – Canada
GB – Great Britain

SU – Soviet Union
BE – Belgium
GR – Greece
FR – France
DE – Germany
IT – Italy
JP – Japan
BG – Bulgaria
RO – Romania
HU – Hungary
FI – Finland
EG – Egypt
PL – Poland
NO – Norway
PH – Philippines
NL – Netherlands

Page 65—First Aid
Answers will vary.

Page 66—Three of a Kind
Answers will vary.

1950s

Page 67—The Cat in the Hat
The Cat in the Hat rhyming words:
pat, fat, sat, rat, mat, bat, at, that, flat, chat
Hidden Phrases:
1. Cat in the hat
2. fish in the pot
3. wall in the hall
4. Things in the box
5. cake in the tub
6. rug in the hall
7. man in the moon
8. shot in the dark
9. cat in the cradle
10. bird in the bush
11. light in the attic
12. bats in the belfry

Answer Key *(cont.)*

Page 68—TV Families

The Smiths
1. Mother—I Love Lucy
2. Father—The George Burns and Gracie Allen Show
3. Jimmy—Leave it to Beaver
4. Judy—Mickey Mouse Club

The Joneses
1. Susie—Lassie
2. Billy—American Bandstand
3. Father—Dragnet
4. Mother—What's My Line?

Page 69—Fads and Fashions
1. pedal pushers
2. rock 'n' roll
3. dungarees
4. television
5. petticoats
6. hand jive
7. TV dinner
8. drive-in
9. coffee house
10. Mad Magazine
11. saddle shoes
12. Beatniks
13. pencils
14. Frisbee
15. ponytail
16. WD-40
17. penny loafers
18. duck tails
19. Barbie
20. crewcut

Page 70—Popular Music Rebus Writing
1. Chuck Berry
2. "Rock Around the Clock"
3. "Teen Angel"
4. "Sixteen Tons"
5. "Unchained Melody"
6. Fats Domino

7. "Jailhouse Rock"
8. "Tears on My Pillow"
9. "Heartbreak Hotel"
10. "Sixteen Candles"

Page 71—Kids' Stuff
1. Frisbee
2. Mad Magazine
3. Barbie Doll
4. rock 'n' roll
5. TV dinner
6. Hula-Hoop
7. Scrabble
8. *Charlotte's Web*
9. Dr. Seuss
10. Jif peanut butter

Page 72—Sports of All Sorts

Baseball
1. Willie Mays
2. Hank Aaron
3. Mickey Mantle

Football
1. Johnny Unitas
2. Jim Brown
3. Otto Graham

Basketball
1. Wilt Chamberlain
2. Bill Russell
3. Bob Cousy

Soccer
1. Pele

Page 73—Guinness Book of World Records
1. Walt Disney
2. Mark McGwire
3. Donovan Bailey
4. Tara Lipinski
5. Michael Jackson's *Thriller*
6. *The Simpsons*
7. Happy Birthday
8. Charles Shulz's *Peanuts*
9. Bible

10. Madeleine Albright
11. Ronald Reagan
12. Bill Gates
pumpkin—1,061 pounds (477.5 kg)
potato—7 pounds/6ounces (3.3 kg)
strawberry—8.17 ounces (228.8 g)
watermelon—262 pounds (117.9 kg)
green bean—48 3/4 inches (121.9 cm)

Page 74—In the News
1. Billy Graham
2. *Twenty-One*
3. Bess Truman
4. Gen. Douglas MacArthur
5. Hawaii
6. Ethel and Julius Rosenberg
7. Rosa Parks
8. 22nd Amendment
9. Korean War
10. Little Rock Nine
11. Althea Gibson
12. Joe DiMaggio
13. *Explorer I*
14. Mary Leakey
15. Buddy Holly, Ritchie Valens, J.P. Richardson

Page 75—Name Game
1. General Douglas Mac Arthur
2. Rosa Parks
3. Linda Brown
4. Louis and Mary Leakey
5. Edmund Hillary, Norgay Tenzing
6. E.B. White
7. Pele
8. Fidel Castro
9. Abdul Nassar
10. Elvis Presley
11. Frank Lloyd Wright
12. Dr. Albert Sabin

Page 76—A Hero from the Fifties
1. source and inspiration for King's nonviolent resistance

2. married King in 1953
3. arrested in 1955 in Montgomery which was catalyst for bus boycott
4. Southern Christian Leadership Conference; organized in 1957 to expand nonviolent struggle against racism; King was the first president.
5. site of protests led by King against segregation and discrimination
6. confessed to assassination of King on April 4, 1968
7. disciple and follower of King; went into politics
8. successor to King as president of SCLC
9. site of protests against restraints on voter registration
10. site where King received the Nobel Peace Prize

Page 77—Alaska and Hawaii
1. H
2. H
3. A
4. A
5. A
6. H
7. H
8. A
9. H
10. H and A
11. A
12. H
13. A
14. H
15. A
16. H
17. A
18. A
19. A
20. H

Answer Key *(cont.)*

Page 78—Happened in the Fifties
1. baby boomers, beat generation
2. Hawaii, Alaska
3. polio vaccine, kidney transplant
4. color television, major league baseball
5. Billy Graham, Pope John XXIII

1960s

Page 79—*Sesame Street*
1. blue
2. yellow
3. Bert
4. Ernie
5. trash
6. numbers
7. red
8. green
9. fun

Page 80—All for Peanuts
1. Snoopy
2. Lucy
3. Woodstock
4. Charlie Brown
5. Peppermint Patty
6. Pig-Pen
7. Linus
8. Schroeder
9. Marcie
10. Sally
Bonus: The little red-haired girl

Page 81—Picture Puzzle

Date: July 20, 1969

Page 82—Beatlemania
1. George Harrison
2. Paul McCartney
3. John Lennon
4. Ringo Starr
Song Titles: "Yellow Submarine," "Love Me Do," "Ticket to Ride," "Penny Lane," "A Hard Day's Night""

Page 83—Popular Music
1. "Moon River"
2. "Yellow Submarine"
3. Ringo Starr
4. Jefferson Airplane
5. "Cathy's Clown"
6. Rolling Stones
7. Woodstock
8. Three Dog Night
9. "California Dreamin'"
10. "I Left My Heart in San Francisco"

Page 84—Double Letters
1. Woodstock
2. Lennon
3. Kennedy
4. assassinated
5. Street
6. Paar
7. Twiggy
8. Missile
9. Poppins
10. guerilla
11. Apollo
12. bullet
13. Dallas
14. wall
15. Frisbee
16. Innsbruck
17. hippies
18. tennis
19. Thurgood Marshall
20. Hollywood

Page 85—The Torch Is Passed
1. afternoon
2. Dallas
3. November 22, 1963
4. rifle
5. riding in a motorcade
6. Jacqueline
7. Lyndon Johnson
8. Lee Harvey Oswald
9. Arlington
10. American
11. John B. Connally
12. convertible

Page 86—Scrambled Names
1. John F. Kennedy
2. Hubert Humphrey
3. Arnold Palmer
4. Gary Powers
5. Floyd Patterson
6. Lyndon B. Johnson
7. Richard Nixon
8. Barry Goldwater
9. Wilma Rudolph
10. Sidney Poitier
11. Alan B. Shepard
12. Bob Dylan
13. Grandma Moses
14. Leonard Bernstein
15. Martin Luther King, Jr.

Page 87—Name Game
1. Richard Milhous Nixon
2. James Earl Ray
3. J. Edgar Hoover
4. John Fitzgerald Kennedy
5. Dwight David Eisenhower
6. Billie Jean King
7. Lee Harvey Oswald
8. Lyndon Baines Johnson
9. Martin Luther King, Jr.
10. Jacqueline Bouvier Kennedy
11. Coretta Scott King

12. Mary Tyler Moore
13. Lady Bird Johnson
14. Norma Jean Baker

Bonus Questions
1. Dwight David Eisenhower, Richard Milhous Nixon, John Fitzgerald Kennedy, Lyndon Baines Johnson
2. Coretta Scott King, Martin Luther King, Jr.
3. Norma Jean Baker
4. Marilyn Monroe

Page 88—Civil Rights Movement
1. Kennedy
2. M.L. King, Jr.
3. 1963
4. Los Angeles
5. nonviolent
6. integration
7. Woolworth's lunch counter
8. bus protest
9. Black Muslim
10. black power
11. Black Panthers
12. Montgomery bus boycott
13. NAACP
14. bombed black churches in the South
15. George Wallace

Answer Key *(cont.)*

Page 89—Fly Me to the Moon
1. F, 1961
2. F, Sputnik
3. F, spacesuits
4. T
5. F, rocks
6. T
7. T
8. T
9. F, Edward White walked outside.
10. F, Florida
11. T
12. F, Saturn
13. F, Neil Armstrong
14. F, days
15. T

Page 90—categories
1. Vietnam War
2. Civil Rights Movement
3. assassinated leaders
4. *Apollo 11* astronauts
5. parts of a microwave oven
6. *Peanuts* cartoon characters
7. Beatles albums
8. Cuban Missile Crisis
9. celebrities born in the 1960s
10. moon landmarks
11. African-American actors
12. subjects of Andy Warhol's paintings
13. Great Society
14. Counterculture Movement
15. popular literary works

Page 91—Analogies
1. Lady Bird
2. prime minister
3. athlete (runner)
4. Washington, D.C.
5. astronaut
6. children's books
7. Israel
8. Charles Schulz
9. Soviet Union

10. Hollywood
11. Rachel Carson
12. surgeon, patient
13. Soviet Union
14. Yuri Gargarin

Page 92—Canada's Centennial
Underline 1,2,5,7,10
1. century
2. centenarian
3. centipede
4. centimeter
5. centigrade
6. centennial
7. centuplicate
8. centuriation
9. centurion
10. percent

Page 93—The Peace Corps

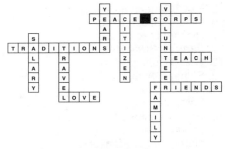

Page 94—African Independence
1. Libya
2. Sudan
3. Morocco
4. Tunisia
5. Ghana
6. Guinea
7. Kenya
8. Cote d'Ivoire
9. Mauritania
10. Malawi
11. Zimbabwe
12. The Gambia

13. Gabon
14. Somalia
15. Egypt
16. Ethiopia
17. Tanzania
18. Mali
19. Senegal
20. Nigeria

1970s

Page 95—Headlines
1. Pierre Trudeau
2. Mark Spitz
3. Spiro Agnew
4. Christo
5. Judy Blume
6. Alex Haley
7. Woody Allen
8. Mikhail Baryshnikov
9. Gloria Steinem
10. Shirley Chisholm
11. Betty Ford
12. Jimmy Carter
13. Richard Nixon
14. Cyrus Vance
15. Michael Spinks, Leon Spinks, Sugar Ray Leonard

Page 96—Food Processors
1. cabbage
2. cheese
3. potatoes
4. onions
5. carrots
6. apples
7. meat
8. dough
9. soup
10. celery

Page 97—Calculator Fun
1. 3504 – hose
2. 304 – hoe
3. 710 – oil

4. 317 – lie
5. 7105 – soil
6. 7718 – Bill
7. 7714 – hill
8. 7735 – sell
9. 618 – big
10. 607 – log
11. 5637 – legs

Page 98—Sydney Opera House
1. Metropolitan Guitar Series
2. wood
3. tires
4. game
5. Great Britain
6. Quebec
7. sand
8. doctor
9. lawyer
10. president

Page 99—Amazon Rain Forest

1. kapok	**Trees**
2. jaguar	1. kapok
3. tapir	2. rubber
4. palm	3. mahogany
5. vines	4. palm
6. cacti	5. banana
7. rubber	**Animals**
8. banana	1. capybara
9. capybara	2. tapir
10. sloth	3. sloth
11. fern	4. armadillo
12. mahogany	5. jaguar
13. armadillo	**Plants**
14. orchid	1. fern
	2. cacti
	3. orchid
	4. vines

Answer Key *(cont.)*

Page 100—Earth Day

1. conserve
2. recycle
3. carbon dioxide
4. oxygen
5. non-biodegradable
6. pollution
7. endangered species
8. energy
9. Styrofoam
10. lights
11. pesticides
12. leak
13. plastic
14. packaging
15. trash

Bonus: environment

Page 101—Words Within Words

1. Vietnam
2. amendment
3. endangered
4. conscription
5. Iran hostage crisis
6. Earth Day
7. environment
8. feminism
9. embargo
10. computer
11. spacecraft
12. fashion
13. Camp David Accord
14. Watergate
15. Affirmative Action

Page 102—Space Exploration

1. F, the command module lost oxygen and the flight returned to Earth.
2. T
3. F, Mars
4. T
5. T
6. F, five years

7. T
8. F, transmitted pictures of Venus and Mercury.
9. T
10. F, discovered rings around Jupiter.

Page 103—Watergate Trivia

1. John Sirica
2. June 17, 1972
3. seven
4. 18 minutes
5. Rose Mary Woods
6. H.R. Haldeman, John Erlichman, Richard Kleindienst, John Dean
7. Carl Bernstein, Bob Woodward
8. Deep Throat
9. Warren Burger
10. obstructing justice
11. He resigned.
12. Gerald Ford
13. Nelson Rockefeller
14. No, Ford pardoned Nixon.
15. They served time in prison.

Page 104—Initials and Acronyms

1. citizens' band radio
2. Committee to Reelect the President
3. Equal Rights Amendment
4. Stratregic Arms Limitation Talks
5. Irish Republican Army
6. computerized axial tomography
7. magnetic resonance imagery
8. personal computer
9. Children's Defense Fund
10. Environmental Protection Agency
11. Organization of Petroleum Exporting Countries
12. National Organization of Women

Page 105—Think Metric

1. 1g
2. 0.001 m
3. 1g
4. 1000 cm³

5. 1g
6. 20–25° C
7. 50° C
8. 35–40° C
9. 10° C
10. 5° C

Page 106—Quebec's Quiet Revolution

School Supplies

scissors
pencil
notebook
glue
colored pencils

Numbers: une, deux, troix, quatre, cinq, six, sept, huit, neuf, dix

Colors: blue, black, brown, green, orange, red, yellow, purple

Common Expressions: thank you, good morning, goodbye, I'm sorry, come in, women, men

Page 107—Who Done It?

1. National Guardsmen
2. Richard M. Nixon
3. Gerald Ford
4. Billie Jean King
5. Jimmy Carter
6. Sony
7. mob of Islamic students
8. Janet Guthrie
9. Steve Cauthen
10. Roberto Clemente
11. Clive Sinclair
12. Henry Heimlich
13. Alex Hale
14. President Carter, Omar Torrijo
15. Arab oil-producing nations

Page 108—R.I.P.

1. Harry S. Truman—1884
2. J. Edgar Hoover—1895
3. Pearl S. Buck—1893

4. Charles Lindbergh—1902
5. Elvis Presley—1935
6. Norman Rockwell—1894
7. Charles De Gaulle—1890
8. Juan Peron—1895
9. Haile Selassie—1892
10. Mao Tse-tung—1893

1980s

Page 109—Olympic People and Places

1. Bonnie Blair
2. Eric Heiden
3. Sarajevo, Yugoslavia
4. Los Angeles, California
5. Lake Placid, New York
6. Moscow, Soviet Union
7. Calgary, Canada
8. Seoul, South Korea
9. Carl Lewis
10. Jackie Joyner-Kersee
11. Mary Lou Retton
12. Janet Evans
13. Greg Louganis
14. Bruce Baumgartner
15. Matt Biondi

Bonus: Afghanistan

Answer Key *(cont.)*

Page 110—Shel Silverstein
1. *The Giving Tree*
2. *Where the Sidewalk Ends*
3. *A Light in the Attic*
4. *Giraffe and a Half*
5. *Falling Up*

rhyming phrases
red and green
sleepy queen
angry teen
fat to lean
beauty queen
old Holstein
never mean
college dean
seldom seen

Page 111—Just a Phone Call Away
1. Mondale
2. Germany
3. Soviets
4. shuttle
5. Live Aid
6. Charles
7. vaccine
8. Madonna
9. nuclear
10. gateway
11. Cold War
12. R. Reagan
13. Chinese
14. scandal

Page 112—*Challenger*
1. tragedy
2. television
3. seal
4. first
5. years
Answer: disaster
Challenge: *Titanic, Lusitania*

Page 113—*Challenger* Shuttle Disaster
1. T
2. T
3. F, there had been nine flights.
4. F, there were seven astronauts.
5. T
6. F, Ronald Reagan was.
7. T
8. F, weather had no effect.

9. T
10. F, NASA knew the seals were a problem.
11. F, the bodies were never found.
12. T

Page 114—Lady Liberty
1. 450,000 pounds
2. 141 feet
3. 8 feet
4. 168 steps
5. 2.5 feet
6. 4.5 feet
7. 42 feet
8. 3 feet
9. 35 feet
"Give me your tired, your poor, Your huddled masses yearning to breathe free. / The wretched refuse of your teeming shore. / Send these, the homeless, tempest-tost to me. / I lift my lamp beside the golden door!"

Page 115—Create a Word
addiction, terrorist, communist, protestor, explosion, hostages, invasion, president, olympics, recycling, barrier, destruction

Page 116—Presidential Puzzle

Page 117—Fabulous Females
1. Sandra Day O'Connor
2. Geraldine Ferraro
3. Margaret Thatcher
4. Nancy Reagan
5. Barbara Bush
6. Wilma Mankiller
7. Indira Gandhi
8. Corazon Aquino
9. Sally Ride
10. Barbara Walters

Page 118—Lists
1. Olympic gold medalists
2. astronauts
3. singers/musicians
4. world leaders
5. famous women
6. disasters
7. Afghanistan
8. Star Wars
9. Iran-Contra
10. Berlin Wall

Page 119—Analogies
1. Lynne Reid Banks
2. New York City
3. Russia/U.S.S.R.
4. movies
5. Mount St. Helens
6. speed skater
7. *Columbia*
8. phone messages
9. Jackson Five
10. Poland
11. Republican
12. Walter Mondale

1990s

Page 120—Techno-Terms
1. software
2. Internet
3. e-mail
4. CD-Rom
5. monitor
6. modem
7. Bill Gates

Page 121—Celebrity Plates
1. Arnold Schwarzenegger
2. Rosie O'Donnell
3. Oprah Winfrey
4. Bill Cosby
5. Tim Allen
6. Michael J. Fox
7. Tom Hanks
8. Will Smith
9. Sylvester Stallone
10-14. Answers may vary.

Page 122—Hilary Clinton Writes
It Takes a Village to Raise a Child

Page 123—The McCaughey Septuplets
Kenneth, Alexis, Kelsey, Natalie, Brandon, Nathan, Joel
septennial—occurring every seven years
septet—a group of seven people
September—seventh month of the Roman calendar
septisyllable—a word with seven syllables
septuagenarian—a person between 70–80 years of age
septuple—to multiply by seven
septuplicate—to copy seven times

Page 124—Michael Jordan *Statistics*

Triple-Double Total		
	1.	23
1. 6'6"	2.	63
2. Juanita	3.	28
3. Deloris	4.	6
4. Jeffrey	5.	5
5. Jasmine	6.	11
6. New York	7.	10
7. University of	8.	29,277
North Carolina	9.	3,041
8. 1984 and 1992	10.	69
9. baseball	11.	45
10. Jeffrey	12.	13
11. Chicago Bulls		
Triple-double total = 28		

Answer Key (cont.)

Page 125—The Right Stuff

10,9,8,7,6,5,4,3,2,1
"Godspeed, John Glenn" was said by fellow astronaut Scott Carpenter.

Page 126—Current Events

1. building of the Eurotunnel
2. German reunification
3. beginning of Gulf War
4. Kremlin coup attempt
5. Gorbachev's resignation
6. World Trade Center bombing

Page 127—Lists

1. Oklahoma City bombing
2. Persian Gulf War/Operation Desert Storm
3. Million Man march
4. joint U.S.-Russian space program
5. Hip Hop/Rap Music
6. Bosnian War
7. fall of U.S.S.R.
8. Palestinian-Israeli Peace Accord
9. end of Apartheid
10. Internet

Page 128—Desert Storm

1. Saudi Arabia
2. Kuwait
3. Iraq
4. Jordan
5. Red Sea
6. Israel
7. United Arab Emirates
8. Persian Gulf
9. Qatar
10. Bahrain

Page 129—Gulf War

1. Operation Desert Storm
2. Saddam Hussein, Norman Schwarzkopf, President George Bush
3. Baghdad; Kuwait; Washington, D.C.

4. scud missile, stealth fighter, Tomahawk cruise missile, combat aircraft

Page 130—Analogies

1. Yale Law School
2. Independent
3. NAACP
4. basketball
5. Microsoft
6. Mississippi
7. Secretary of State
8. Bill Clinton
9. speed skating
10. tennis racket
11. Dan Quayle
12. Israel
13. James Cameron
14. England

Page 131—Web Sites

1. Boris Yeltsin
2. Hillary Clinton
3. Louis Farrakhan
4. Tiger Woods
5. General Colin Powell
6. Janet Reno
7. Ross Perot
8. Michael Jordan
9. Bill Gates
10. Shannon Lucid
11. Oprah Winfrey
12. Yitzhak Rabin
13. Nelson Mandela
14. Mikhail Gorbachev
15. Yasir Arafat

Page 132—Initials and Acronyms

1. Union of Soviet Socialist Republics
2. Palestine Liberation Organization
3. United Nation
4. African National Congress
5. compact disk read-only memory
6. double income no kids
7. World-Wide Web

8. North Atlantic Treaty Organization
9. Microsoft Disk Operating System
10. National Aeronautic and Space Administration
11. International Business Machines
12. Professional Golfer's Association
13. National Association for the Advancement of Colored People
14. Reserve Officers Training Corps
15. Electronic Data Systems

General Section

Page 133— Top Ten Best Selling Children's Books

Hardcover

10. *One Fish, Two Fish, Red Fish, Blue Fish*
9. *The Littlest Angel*
8. *The Cat in the Hat*
7. *Green Eggs and Ham*
6. *Pat the Bunny*
5. *Scuffy the Tugboat*
4. *Saggy Baggy Elephant*
3. *Tootle*
2. *The Tale of Peter Rabbit*
1. *The Poky Little Puppy*

Paperback

10. *Little House in the Big Woods*
9. *Little House on the Prairie*
8. *Island of the Blue Dolphins*
7. *A Wrinkle in Time*
6. *Where the Red Fern Grows*
5. *Are You There God? It's Me, Margaret*
4. *Shane*
3. *Tales of a Fourth Grade Nothing*
2. *The Outsiders*
1. *Charlotte's Web*

Page 134—Popular Pairs

1. Hardy
2. Jerry
3. Olive Oyl
4. Minnie
5. Beast

6. Jeff
7. Tramp
8. Cher
9. Gromit
10. Tweety Bird
11. Tonto
12. Ken
13. Jethro
14. Shirley
15. Mindy
16. Robin
17. Lois Lane
18. Hutch
19. Desi
20. Harriet

Page 135—Famous Pairs

1. Mary and Louis Leakey
2. Hans and Margaret Reyser
3. Juan and Evita Peron
4. Julius and Ethel Rosenberg
5. George Burns and Gracie Allen
6. Franklin and Eleanor Roosevelt
7. George and Ira Gershwin
8. Robert Peary and Matthew Henson
9. Ronald and Nancy Reagan
10. Charles and Diana
11. Mairead Corrigan and Betty Williams
12. General George Goethals and General William Gorgas

Page 136—O Canada

1. Great Bear Lake (shape)
2. Great Goose Lake (name & shape)
3. Little Goose Lake (name & shape)
4. Saskatchewan (spelling)
5. Manitoba (spelling)
6. Baffin Bay (Hudson Bay)
7. Hudson Bay (Ungava Bay)
8. Quebec (spelling)
9. Sir Lawrence Seaway (Saint Lawrence . . .)
10. King Edward Island (Prince Edward . . .)

Answer Key (cont.)

Page 137—Famous Canadians
Prime Ministers
1. Brian Mulroney
2. Pierre Trudeau
3. Jean Chretien
TV and Movie Stars
1. William Shatner
2. Michael J. Fox
3. Matthew Perry
Athletes
1. Wayne Gretzky
2. Anne Pelletier
3. Donovan Bailey
Female Astronaut—Roberta Bonday
Popular Music Stars
1. Celine Dion
2. Shania Twain
3. Alanis Morisette
Marathon of Hope
1. Terry Fox

Page 138—This Land Is Your Land
1. Oregon (spelling)
2. Rocky Mountains (place)
3. Appalachian Mountains (place)
4. Nevada (spelling)
5. Arizona (spelling)
6. Grand Canyon (place)
7. Rio Grande R. (place)
8. Mississippi R. (place)
9. Minnesota (spelling)
10. Missouri (spelling)
11. Arkansas (spelling)
12. Mississippi (spelling)
13. Tennessee (spelling)
14. Pennsylvania (spelling)
15. Virginia (spelling)
16. Connecticut (spelling)

Page 139—Man-made World Landmarks
1. Kansai Airport
2. Sydney Opera House
3. Aswan High Dam

4. Channel Tunnel
5. CN Tower
6. Golden Gate Bridge
7. Hoover Dam (Boulder Canyon Project)
8. Panama Canal
9. Seikan Tunnel
10. Mount Rushmore

Page 140—Australian Animals
Australian Animals
1. platypus
2. echidna
3. dingo
4. wombat
5. wallaby
6. koala
7. bandicoot
8. emu
9. kookaburra
10. cassowary
11. Tasmanian Devil
12. camel

Page 141—Picture the Presidents
1. Bush
2. Carter
3. Hayes
4. Grant
5. Pierce
6. Taylor
7. Polk
8. Tyler

Page 142—Quotes and Slogans
1. Eisenhower
2. F.D. Roosevelt
3. Johnson
4. Teddy Roosevelt
5. McKinley
6. Ford
7. Truman
8. Reagan
9. Bush
10. Clinton

Page 143—Nicknames
1. Babe Ruth
2. Pele
3. Dwight Eisenhower
4. Ronald Reagan
5. Bill Cosby
6. Margaret Thatcher
7. Johnny Carson
8. Jack Nicklaus
9. Thomas Edison
10. Bill Clinton
11. Louis Armstrong
12. Ty Cobb
13. Charlie Chaplin
14. Mary Pickford
15. Al Capone

Page 144—Web Sites
1. tennis
2. soccer
3. Mount Saint Helens
4. *Exxon Valdez*
5. Berlin Wall
6. George Washington Carver, Booker T. Washington
7. Norman Rockwell
8. Wilma Mankiller
9. Sydney Opera House
10. Neil Armstrong
11. Pope John Paul II
12. Sandra Day O'Connor
13. Lyndon Johnson
14. Watergate
15. Beatles

Page 145—Equations
1. players on a baseball team
2. students integrating Little Rock Central High School
3. presidents on Mount Rushmore
4. students killed at Kent State University
5. Japanese Americans confined during World War II
6. states in the United States

7. legal age to vote in the U.S.
8. Americans died in the Vietnam War
9. Beatles recorded rock and roll music
10. countries in the United Nations
11. times John Glenn orbited Earth
12. John Fitzgerald Kennedy's age when elected president
13. times Franklin Delano Roosevelt elected president
14. years Germany was divided by the Berlin Wall
15. Allied Powers in World War II

Pages 146 and 147—Fashion Show
1. 1920s
2. 1950s
3. 1940s
4. 1900s
5. 1970s
6. 1960s and/or 1970s

Page 148—R.I.P.
1. Carrie Nation-1911
2. Beatrix Potter-1943
3. Ty Cobb-1961
4. Mary Pickford-1979
5. Buffalo Bill Cody-1917
6. Charlie Chaplin-1977
7. Amelia Earhart-1937
8. Jackie Robinson-1972
9. Evita Peron-1952
10. Gracie Allen-1964